The Teachings of the Essenes

from Enoch

to the

Dead Sea Scrolls

by

EDMOND BORDEAUX SZEKELY

LONDON
THE C. W. DANIEL CO. LTD

First published in Great Britain
by The C. W. Daniel Co., Ltd.,
60 Muswell Road, London, N.10 2BE

Previously published in the U.S.A. 1977

SBN 85207 141 8

5-87

Printed and bound in Great Britain by
Billing & Sons Ltd., Guildford, London and Worcester

Preface

The several chapters of this book are compiled from material antedating the findings of the Dead Sea Scrolls in 1947. During the twenty preceding years, 1927 to 1947, I wrote and published a number of books on the Essenes based on certain historical sources such as the works of Josephus Flavius, Philo and Plinius, and on manuscripts in the Library of the Vatican, the Library of the Habsburgs in Vienna and the Library of the British Museum. In these books I concentrated on the Essene traditions which I consider of great practical value for modern man.

When the first discoveries at Qumrum became public and many persons urged me to publish an interpretation of these new findings, I decided to do so in two volumes. This first volume condenses the quintessence of the Essene traditions from pre-Qumrum sources. The second volume will deal exclusively with the new discoveries.

The present work is concerned with the meaning of the Essene traditions in relation to their values for mankind today and the actual practices which result in an expansion of consciousness. These values may be considered from four standpoints.

1. The Essene traditions represent a synthesis of the great contributions to humanity of the different cultures of antiquity.

2. They represent for us a path leading away from the one-sided utilitarian technology of contemporary civilization, a valid and practical teaching utilizing all the sources of energy, harmony and knowledge everywhere surrounding us.

3. They give us permanent standards in an age where truth seems to dissolve in a continual shifting of concepts.

4. This resulting neurosis and insecurity is given a complete balance and harmony through the Essene teachings.

It is noteworthy that in his book, "The Meaning of the Dead Sea Scrolls," A. Powell Davies says of the Essenes, "The Christian Church in its organization, its sacraments, its teaching and its literature is related to—and in its early stages may have been identical with—the New Covenanters, who were known as Essenes, some of whom wrote the Dead Sea Scrolls."

Likewise significant in the pre-Qumrum traditions of the Essenes is the existence of certain Zoroastrian elements, a fact which I have previously maintained and which Arnold Toynbee has also pointed out in a recent writing. They bear a similar correlation to later teachings like those of the Kabala and Freemasonry. Their most unique element, which has apparently been developed independently, is their science of Angelology.

The quotations appearing on the page preceding each chapter are from two of the Dead Sea Scrolls, the "Manual of Discipline" and the "Thanksgiving Psalms," or "Book of Hymns," which I have translated from photostatic copies of the original texts found in the caves of Qumrum.

Edmond Bordeaux Szekely

San Diego, California, 1957

CONTENTS

"The Law was planted in the garden of the
    Brotherhood
to enlighten the heart of man
and to make straight before him
all the ways of true righteousness,
a humble spirit, an even temper,
a freely compassionate nature,
and eternal goodness and understanding and insight,
and mighty wisdom which believes in all God's
    works
and a confident trust in His many blessings
and a spirit of knowledge in all things of the Great
    Order,
loyal feelings toward all the children of truth,
a radiant purity which loathes everything impure,
a discretion regarding all the hidden things of truth
and secrets of inner knowledge."

From "The Manual of Discipline"
of the Dead Sea Scrolls

INTRODUCTION

The decision to republish this book in Britain is greatly to be welcomed. Dr. Szekely has given us the wonderful volume *The Gospel of the Essenes* (1976), the result of ten years of work in translating and bringing together the essence of Essene teaching from the ancient scrolls. It is a beautiful and inspiring work, poetical and scriptural, and unburdened with academic notes. But there is a vital need for a key to guide the reader and interpret the Communions with the Angels of Earth and Heaven, for without this he may feel somewhat lost in the splendid biblical poetry. This key is provided in the earlier book *From Enoch to the Dead Sea Scrolls*. I warmly recommend every reader of the *Gospel* to take this admirable and concise statement of the Essene teaching and use it as a commentary on the main volume. The *Gospel* can then be richly used as an instrument for meditation, since its inspiration is directly applicable to the needs of our own time and 'speaks to our condition'.

Sir George Trevelyan

And Enoch walked with God;
and he was not;
for God took him.

Genesis 5:24

Chapter 1

The Essenes and Their Teaching

From the remote ages of antiquity a remarkable teaching has existed which is universal in its application and ageless in its wisdom. Fragments of it are found in Sumerian hieroglyphs and on tiles and stones dating back some eight or ten thousand years. Some of the symbols, such as for the sun, moon, air, water and other natural forces, are from an even earlier age preceding the cataclysm that ended the Pleistocene period. How many thousands of years previous to that the teaching existed is unknown.

To study and practice this teaching is to reawaken within the heart of every man an intuitive knowledge that can solve his individual problems and the problems of the world.

Traces of the teaching have appeared in almost every country and religion. Its fundamental principles were taught in ancient Persia, Egypt, India, Tibet, China, Palestine, Greece and many other countries. But it has been transmitted in its most pure form by the Essenes, that mysterious brotherhood which lived during the last two or three centuries B. C. and the first century of the Christian era at the Dead Sea in Palestine and at Lake Mareotis in Egypt. In Palestine and Syria the members of the brotherhood were known as Essenes and in Egypt as Therapeutae, or healers.

The esoteric part of their teaching is given in The Tree of Life, The Communions, and the Sevenfold Peace. The exoteric or outer teaching appears in "The Essene Gospel of John," "Genesis, An Essene Interpretation," "Moses, the Prophet of the Law," and "The Sermon on the Mount."

The origin of the brotherhood is said to be unknown, and the derivation of the name is uncertain. Some believe it comes from Esnoch, or Enoch, and claim him to be their founder, their Communion with the angelic world having first been given to him.

Others consider the name comes from Esrael, the elects of the people to whom Moses brought forth the Communions at Mount Sinai where they were revealed to him by the angelic world.

But whatever their origin, it is certain the Essenes existed for a very long time as a brotherhood, perhaps under other names in other lands.

The teaching appears in the Zend Avesta of Zoroaster, who translated it into a way of life that was followed for thousands of years. It contains the fundamental concepts of Brahmanism, the Vedas and the Upanishads; and the Yoga systems of India sprang from the same source. Buddha later gave forth essentially the same basic ideas and his sacred Bodhi tree is correlated with the Essene Tree of Life. In Tibet the teaching once more found expression in the Tibetan Wheel of Life.

The Pythagoreans and Stoics in ancient Greece also followed the Essene principles and much of their way of life. The same teaching was an element of the Adonic culture of the Phoenicians, of the Alexandrian School of Philosophy in Egypt, and contributed greatly to many branches of Western culture, Freemasonry, Gnosticism, the Kabala and Christianity. Jesus interpreted it in its most sublime and beautiful form in the seven Beatitudes of the Sermon on the Mount.

The Essenes lived on the shores of lakes and rivers, away from cities and towns, and practiced a communal way of life, sharing equally in everything. They were mainly agriculturists and arboriculturists, having a vast knowledge of crops, soil and climatic conditions which enabled them to grow a great variety of fruits and vegetables in comparatively desert areas and with a minimum of labor.

They had no servants or slaves and were said to have been the first people to condemn slavery both in theory and practice. There were no rich and no poor amongst them, both conditions being considered by them as deviations from the Law. They established their own economic system, based wholly on the Law, and showed that all man's food and material needs can be attained without struggle, through knowledge of the Law.

They spent much time in study both of ancient writings and special branches of learning, such as education, healing and astronomy. They were said to be the heirs of Chaldean and Persian astronomy and Egyptian arts of healing. They were adept in prophecy for which they prepared by prolonged fasting. In the use of plants and herbs for healing man and beast they were likewise proficient.

They lived a simple regular life, rising each day before sunrise to study and commune with the forces of nature, bathing in cold water as a ritual and donning white garments. After their daily labor in the fields and vineyards they partook of their meals in silence, preceding and ending it with prayer. They were entirely vegetarian in their eating and never touched flesh foods nor fermented liquids. Their evenings were devoted to study and communion with the heavenly forces.

Evening was the beginning of their day and their Sabbath or holy day began on Friday evening, the first day of their week. This day was given to study, discussion, the entertaining of visitors and playing certain musical instruments, replicas of which have been found.

Their way of life enabled them to live to advanced ages of 120 years or more and they were said to have marvelous strength and endurance. In all their activities they expressed creative love.

They sent out healers and teachers from the brotherhoods, amongst whom were Elijah, John the Baptist, John the Beloved and the great Essene Master, Jesus.

Membership in the brotherhood was attainable only

after a probationary period of a year and three years of initiatory work, followed by seven more years before being given the full inner teaching.

Records of the Essene way of life have come down to us from writings of their contemporaries. Pliny, the Roman naturalist, Philo the Alexandrian philosopher, Josephus the Jewish historian and soldier, Solanius and others spoke of them variously as "a race by themselves, more remarkable than any other in the world," "the oldest of the initiates, receiving their teaching from Central Asia," "teaching perpetuated through an immense space of ages," "constant and unalterable holiness."

Some of the outer teaching is preserved in Aramaic text in the Vatican in Rome. Some in Slavic text was found in the possession of the Habsburgs in Austria and said to have been brought out of Asia in the thirteenth century by Nestorian priests fleeing the hordes of Genghis Khan.

Echoes of the teaching exist today in many forms, in rituals of the Masons, in the seven-branched candlestick, in the greeting "Peace be with you," used from the time of Moses.

From its antiquity, its persistence through the ages, it is evident the teaching could not have been the concept of any individual or any people, but is the interpretation, by a succession of great Teachers, of the Law of the universe, the basic Law, eternal and unchanging as the stars in their courses, the same now as two or ten thousand years ago, and as applicable today as then.

The teaching explains the Law, shows how man's deviations from it are the cause of all his troubles, and gives the method by which he can find his way out of his dilemma.

Thou hast made known unto me
Thy deep, mysterious things.
All things exist by Thee
and there is none beside Thee.
By Thy Law
Thou hast directed my heart
that I set my steps straight forward
upon right paths
and walk where Thy presence is.

From the Book of Hymns **VII**
of the Dead Sea Scrolls

The Law was planted to reward the children of Light
with healing and abundant peace,
with long life,
with fruitful seed of everlasting blessings,
with eternal joy
in immortality of eternal Light.

From "The Manual of Discipline"
of the Dead Sea Scrolls

Chapter 2

The One Law

The teachings which Moses brought forth at Mount Sinai were practiced fifteen hundred years later by the Essene Brotherhoods in Palestine and Egypt.

To understand his teachings is to understand the values the Essene practices have for man today.

Moses was the giver of the Law, the One Law. He established the monotheism that was to become not only the fundamental tenet of the Essene Brotherhoods but of all western civilization. The most authoritative information we have about his teaching comes from their Brotherhoods.

Their tradition divides his life into three periods symbolic of the experiences in every man's life. In the first period of forty years, during which he lived as a prince of Egypt, he followed the path of tradition, acquiring all the education and knowledge available. He studied the rituals of Isis, Amon-Ra and Osiris, the Precepts of Pta Hotep, the Egyptian Book of the Dead, and traditions that came from the East to Egypt, the cultural center of the world at that time. But in all his studying he found no inner dynamism or unifying principle explaining the universe and the problems of life.

In the second period of his life he spent forty years in the desert following the path of nature, studying the book of nature, as have many other great geniuses and prophets, including Jesus. In the huge vastnesses of the desert, with their solitude and silence, great inner truths have been brought forth. In this period of his life Moses discovered the One Law, the totality of all laws. He found that this one Law governed all manifestations of life, and it governed the whole universe. To him it was the greatest of all miracles to find that everything operates under one law. Then he came upon the idea of the totality of laws. And this totality he called the Law, spelled with a capital "L."

17

He first observed that man lives in a dynamic, constantly changing universe; plants and animals grow and disappear; moons wax and wane. There is no static point in nature or man. He saw that the Law manifests in perpetual change, and that behind the change is a plan of Cosmic Order on a vast scale.

He came to understand that the Law is the greatest and only power in the universe and that all other laws and all things are a part of the one Law. The Law is subject to no other law or laws. It is eternal, indestructible, incapable of defeat. A plant, a tree, a human body or a solar system each has its own laws, mathematical, biological and astronomical. But the one supreme power, the Law, is behind all of them.

The Law governs all that takes place in the universe, and all other universes, all activity, all creation, mental or physical. It governs all that exists in physical manifestation, in energy and power, in consciousness, all knowledge, all thought, all feeling, all reality. The Law creates life and it creates thought.

The sum total of life on all the planets in the universe was called by the Essenes the cosmic ocean of life. And the sum total of currents of thought in the universe was called the cosmic ocean of thought, or cosmic consciousness in more modern terminology.

This cosmic ocean of life and cosmic ocean of thought form a dynamic unity of which man is an inseparable part. Every thinking body of every individual is in constant inner communion with this unity. Every human being is an individualized part of the unity. This unity is the Law, the Eternal Light, of which Moses spoke.

Moses saw the Law broken everywhere. Egypt had been built without regard for it. Despite the nation's great military and political might, there was no law of equality. Misery and slavery existed everywhere; rich and poor alike suffered from oppression, epidemics and plagues. He learned that ignorance of the Law, of the laws of nature, was responsible for all evils, and that the rulers and the ruled were equally to blame.

It became evident to Moses that everything created as a result of deviation from the Law destroys itself and in time disappears. Only the Law is eternal.

The third period of Moses' life, the Exodus, began when he determined to dedicate the remainder of his days to the realization and application of the Law, and to bringing mankind into harmony with it. He recognized the enormity of the task before him in attempting to make both the ignorant masses and the arrogant rulers accept the Law and live in harmony with it. Seemingly insurmountable obstacles confront all world reformers, when pure idea meets the opposing force in the inertia of the human mind and the resistance of entrenched power. It represents a revolution of the dynamic against the static, of higher values against pseudo-values, of freedom against slavery, and it is not limited to one time in history, nor to mankind as a whole, but occurs repeatedly in the life of individual man.

When Moses found he could not change the Egyptian rulers or the masses of the people, he turned to the small minority, the enslaved and oppressed people of Israel, hoping to convert them and establish a new nation based wholly on the Law. He is the only figure in universal history that did establish such a nation.

Moses saw the universe as a gigantic Cosmic Order in which existed inexhaustible sources of energy, knowledge and harmony at man's disposal. He had always remembered the two legends of his ancestor Jacob who had fought and conquered an angel and later had had a vision of angels ascending and descending upon a ladder connecting heaven and earth. He identified these angels as the forces of nature and the powers of man's consciousness and saw that these forces and powers were the connecting link between man and God. He identified God with the great universal Law.

He came to the conclusion that if man is to reach God, he must first become master of all the forces which are manifestations of God, of the Law. He wanted to make his people "strong with the Law," which is the meaning of the word Israel. And he wanted to create a system of life which would make it possible for them to conquer the angels as their forefather, Jacob, had done. This was the foundation of occult science as it is termed today, of the science of the angels, later recorded as angelology.

Moses wanted his followers to realize that they are in constant contact, every moment of their lives and in all points of their being, with all the forces of life and the visible and invisible universe; and if they contact these powers consciously, and become continually conscious of them, they will enjoy perfect health, happiness and harmony in body and mind and every department of their lives.

The method of contacting these forces was engraved on the two stone tablets he brought down from Mt. Sinai but destroyed when he found the masses of his people were not ready for the teaching, even as the masses of mankind are not ready for it today and may not be for many generations to come. But to the few who were ready he taught the method given on the tablets, the Communions with the angels, which has been preserved through the ages in the Essene Brotherhoods and can still be practiced by man today.

This was a part of the esoteric teaching given by Moses and practiced in the Essene Brotherhoods five centuries preceding the Christian era.

In later Essene traditions the abstract idea of the Law was conveyed by the symbol of a tree, called the Tree of Life. Moses had received a great revelation when he saw the burning bush in the desert. This represented two aspects of universal life: warmth and light. The warmth of the fire symbolized the fire of life, vitality in the material world. The light, symbolizing man's consciousness, represented the light of wisdom as opposed to the darkness of ignorance in the immaterial universe. Together they represent the whole universe and the idea that man in the center draws life and vitality from all the forces of the cosmos.

The Essenes symbolized this teaching in their Tree of Life which pictured to them in a concrete form that man was a unity of energy, thoughts and emotions and a unit of life force constantly communing with the totality of energies in the universe. Moses wished to see man living in harmony with the laws which govern all these energies inside and outside man, and to become conscious of them and utilize them in every moment of life.

In his study of the totality of the Law Moses attained an intuitive knowledge of the origin of the world and the beginning of all things. It was from this beginning of all things he derived the laws for daily life. He learned that all things are parts of the whole, put together according to law; and the seven elements or basic forces of life appeared in seven great cycles of creation, one element in each cycle. He grouped the days of the week into a corresponding cycle of seven, considering each day to correspond to a different one of the elements. This was symbolized in Essene traditions by the seven-branched candlestick, the candles of which were lit every seventh day, the sabbath, to remind man of the seven cycles and the seven basic forces of the visible world and the seven basic powers of the invisible world of man's consciousness.

The three periods of Moses' life, in which he discovered the Law and its manifestations, represent the three periods into which nearly every man's life can be divided. The first, Egypt, has been called the period of bondage, of the darkness of ignorance, when the free flow of vital energy is obstructed by ignorance and false values. Mankind's Egypt, his slavery, consists in the totality of his deviations from the Law.

The second period in Moses' life corresponds to the desert in an individual's life when his false values fall away· and he sees nothing but emptiness ahead of him. It is in this period man most urgently needs inner guidance that he may find his way back to the Light, the Law.

The third period, the Exodus, is possible for every man. There is always the Light showing the way to the exodus. Man's Egypt of bondage is never eternal. The Exodus under Moses lasted forty years, but it was only a beginning on the path of intuition, the path of learning to live in harmony with the laws of life, of nature and the cosmos. An exodus for humanity can only be accomplished through the cumulative efforts of many people over many generations.

But it can be accomplished and it will be accomplished. There is always a Canaan, which is not a mythical utopia, but a living reality. The exodus is the path that leads toward Canaan, the path that Moses trod, the path to which the Essene practices light the way.

"I thank Thee, Heavenly Father,
because Thou hast put me
at a source of running streams,
at a living spring in a land of drought,
watering an eternal garden of wonders,
the Tree of Life, mystery of mysteries,
growing everlasting branches for eternal planting
to sink their roots into the stream of life
from an eternal source.

"And Thou, Heavenly Father,
protect their fruits
with the angels of the day
and of the night
and with flames of eternal Light burning every way."

From the "Thanksgiving Psalms"
of the Dead Sea Scrolls
VIII (viii. 4-12)

Chapter 3

The Essene Tree of Life

Man has appeared to realize, as far back as records exist, that he was surrounded by invisible forces. In culture after culture of the past he has used a certain symbolism to express his relationship to these forces in the midst of which he moves. This mystical symbol which has been imbedded in almost all religions and occult teachings is called the Tree of Life. In outer legend and inner wisdom man's deepest intuitions have focussed about it.

It was considered by Zoroaster as the law itself and was the center of his philosophy and way of thinking. In the hidden teachings of Moses, the Essene Book of Genesis, it was the Tree of Knowledge in the Garden of Eden guarded by angels. The Essenes called it the Tree of Life.

To the earlier concepts of the Tree the Essenes added what the ancient writers called Angelology. This Science of the Angels was brought forth by the Essenes at their brotherhood in Palestine. Their angels were the forces in the universe.

It was known by many of the ancient peoples that these invisible forces were a source of energy and power, and that man's life was sustained by contact with them. They knew that to the degree man was able to utilize these forces, he would move forward in his individual evolution in body and spirit, and as he put himself in harmony with them, his life would prosper. Certain of the people not only knew of these forces but had specific methods of contacting and utilizing them.

In many lands these forces were considered to be of two kinds, good and evil, and eternally opposed to each other. Zoroaster in his Zend Avesta described the Ahuras and Fravashis as the good forces forever battling with the evil Khrafstras and Devas. The Toltecs in Mexico and Central America held a world picture in which the good forces were called the Army of Quetzalcoatl, the Plumed Serpent, and the evil forces were the Army of Tezcatlipoca, the Jaguar. These two armies were shown in the Toltec pictographs as being in continual conflict with each other. In the Zoroastrian and Toltec concepts destructive forces were always fighting the constructive ones.

The concept of the Essenes differed from these and other world pictures in that it recognized only the positive and constructive forces in the universe. The Essene angels correspond to the good forces of Zoroaster, the Ahuras and Fravashis, and to the good forces of the Toltecs, the Army of Quetzalcoatl. It was held to be man's role in the universe to so strengthen the good, positive forces that the evil negative ones would be overcome and disappear from the earth.

The Essene Tree of Life represented fourteen positive forces, seven of them heavenly or cosmic forces and seven earthly or terrestrial forces. The Tree was pictured as having seven roots reaching down into the earth and seven branches extending up toward the heavens, thus symbolizing man's relationship to both earth and heaven. Man was pictured in the center of the tree half-way between heaven and earth.

The use of the number seven is an intregal part of the Essene tradition which has been transmitted to Western cultures in various outer ways, such as the seven days of the week.

Each root and branch of the tree represented a different force or power. The roots represented earthly forces and powers, the Earthly Mother, the Angel of Earth, the Angel of Life, the Angel of Joy, the Angel of the Sun, the Angel of Water and the Angel of Air. The seven branches represented cosmic powers, The Heavenly Father, and his Angels of Eternal Life, Creative Work, Peace, Power, Love and Wisdom. These were the Essene angels of the visible and invisible worlds.

In ancient Hebrew and Medieval literature these heavenly and earthly forces or angels were given names, Michael, Gabriel and so on; and they were pictured in religious art as human figures with wings and clad in flowing robes, such as in the frescoes of Michael Angelo.

Man, in the center of the Tree, was seen to be surrounded as in a magnetic field, by all the forces, or angels, of heaven and earth. He was pictured as in the meditation posture, the upper half of his body above the ground and the lower half in the earth. This indicated that part of man is allied to the forces of heaven and part to the forces of earth. This concept closely parallels that of Zoroaster who represented the universe as a framework of realms with man in its center and the various forces above and below him. It also corresponds to the Toltec ritual performed on the steps of their pyramids with man in the midst of all the forces.

This position of man in the center of the Tree, with the earthly forces below him and the heavenly forces above, also corresponds to the position of the organs in the physical body. The gastric and generative tracts in the lower half of the body, being instruments of self-preservation and self-perpetuation, belong to the earthly forces. Whereas the lungs and brain, in the upper half of the body, are the instruments of breathing and thinking and thus connect man with the finer forces of the universe.

Contact with the angelic forces represented by the Tree of Life was the very essence of the daily life of the Essenes. They knew that to be in harmony with these forces they must make conscious effort to contact them. The Essenes were spoken of by the ancient writers as an extremely practical people. Their concepts were not just theories; they knew exactly how to be continually aware of the forces about them and how to absorb their power and put them into action in their daily lives.

They had the deep wisdom to understand that these forces were sources of energy, knowledge and harmony by which man can transform his organism into a more and more sensitive instrument to receive and consciously utilize the forces. Furthermore, they considered that to put himself into harmony with the forces of the Heavenly Father and the Earthly Mother was man's most important activity in life.

The characteristics of each one of the different forces was very clear to them and they knew what the force meant in each individual's life and how it should be utilized.

They also understood the relationship between the forces. They considered that each heavenly force has an earthly force corresponding to it and each earthly force a corresponding heavenly power. These corresponding heavenly and earthly forces were placed on the Essene Tree of Life diagonally across from each other, one above and one below man. A line drawn between any two corresponding forces consequently passed directly through man in the center of the Tree.

The forces which correspond with each other, above and below, are as follows:

The Heavenly Father and the Earthly Mother

The Angel of Eternal Life and the Angel of Earth

The Angel of Creative Work and the Angel of Life

The Angel of Peace and the Angel of Joy

The Angel of Power and the Angel of the Sun

The Angel of Love and the Angel of Water

The Angel of Wisdom and the Angel of Air

These correlations showed the Essenes that when an individual contacts any earthly force he is also in touch with a certain heavenly power. This enabled them to understand how necessary it is to be in perfect harmony with each and every one of the forces and angels, both in the visible and invisible worlds.

The symbolical Tree of Life made it clear to the people how inseparably they are linked to all the forces, cosmic and terrestrial, and it showed them what their relationship is to each.

"I am grateful, Heavenly Father,
for Thou hast raised me to an eternal height
and I walk in the wonders of the plain.

"Thou gavest me guidance to reach Thine eternal
*   company*
from the depths of the earth.

"Thou hast purified my body
to join the army of the angels of the earth
and my spirit to reach
the congregation of the heavenly angels.

"Thou gavest man eternity
to praise at dawn and dusk
Thy works and wonders
in joyful song."

From the "Thanksgiving Psalms"
of the Dead Sea Scrolls
VI (iii, 19-36)

Chapter 4

The Essene Communions

I — THEIR PURPOSE AND MEANING

The symbolic Tree of Life enabled the Essenes to understand how they were surrounded by forces, or angels, from the visible world of nature and the invisible cosmic world. The Communions show how each of these forces is utilized in man's body and consciousness.

The Communions are said to have been originated by Esnoch, or Enoch, and were again brought forth by Moses to Esrael, the elect of the people, on the two stone tablets he first brought down from Mount Sinai. The second set of tablets he brought down contained the Ten Commandments, the outer teaching, which he gave to the rest of the people, Israel. But the small minority, Esrael, or the Essenes, from that time on, held their communions morning and evening, to the earthly and heavenly forces, regulating their lives according to the inspiration received from them.

The Communions have three immediate objectives.

The first is to make man conscious of the activities of the different forces and forms of energy which surround him and perpetually flow toward him from nature and the cosmos.

The second is to make him aware of the organs and centers within his being which can receive these currents of energy.

The third is to establish a connection between the organs and centers and their corresponding forces so as to absorb, control and utilize each current.

The Essenes knew that man has different bodily systems to absorb the different energies from food, air, water, solar radiations and so on; and they knew that each individual must control and utilize these powers for himself through his own conscious efforts, and that no one could do it for him.

The Communions were practiced each morning and evening, a different earthly force being meditated upon each morning upon arising, and a different heavenly force each evening before retiring, each day of the week. This made a total of fourteen communions during each seven day period.

At each of the Communions the designated force was concentrated upon, contemplated and meditated upon so that its power could be absorbed and consciously utilized in whatever intensity was required.

An explanation of the purpose of each Communion follows:

THE MORNING COMMUNIONS

The Earthly Mother—Saturday Morning

The purpose of this Communion was to establish unity between man's physical organism and the nutritive forces of the earth.

This was accomplished by contemplating the different food substances and realizing that the body is formed of the elements of the earth, and is nourished with those elements through plant life. This teaches the meaning and importance of the natural foods of the earth supplied by the Earthly Mother in harmony with the laws governing terrestrial life. Through this man learns of the paramount role of natural foods in his health and vitality and he becomes conscious of the processes of metabolism within him. He learns, furthermore, how to receive and absorb the powerful energies derived from foods and how to conserve those energies in his body. He thus gradually develops the ability to assimilate perfectly and utilize all the nutritive substances he eats and the energies in them; thus he is able to derive more sustenance from a given amount of food.

This Communion was one of the principal instruments by which the Essenes maintained such remarkable physical health.

The Angel of Earth—Sunday Morning

The Earthly Mother's Angel of Earth was the power of generation and regeneration. A central idea of the Essenes, similar to that of Zoroaster, was to create more and more abundant life. The purpose of the Communion was to transform the generative powers in life into the regeneration of the human body. They conceived this power in man to be the same natural force as the generative powers of nature in the top soil, which creates the vegetation of the earth.

This Communion therefore relates to the surface of the earth where things germinate, and to the power of fertility and the glands and organs of generation. It taught the importance of the life-generating powers of the soil and of the regenerative force of sexual energy in the glandular system. It made man conscious of the life generating forces in and around him, enabling him to be more receptive in absorbing this great power, and mastering, directing and utilizing it.

The Essenes' extraordinary faculty of self-regeneration was primarily due to their transforming sexual energy through the practice of this Communion.

The Angel of Life—Monday Morning

This Communion was dedicated to the life, health and vitality of the human organism and that of the whole planet and brought about a dynamic unity between them.

It taught man the role of vitality in his well being and made him conscious of all the innumerable activities of the life force in and around him, enabling him to direct it to any part of his body in the intensity required.

It gave the Essenes their astonishing ability to absorb life force especially from trees and forests.

The Angel of Joy—Tuesday Morning

All forms of beauty were joyously contemplated in this Communion in order to make man conscious of the beauties of nature and the joy within himself in every part of his being.

This faculty of absorbing joy from the beauties of nature, sunrises, sunsets, mountains, flowers, colors, aromas and so on was one of the means by which the Essenes attained the inner harmony and serenity which so impressed their contemporaries.

The Angel of the Sun—Wednesday morning

The Essenes meditated on the Sun as a great living force in terrestrial nature, an ever-present source of energy without which there would be no life on earth, in the ocean or in the atmosphere. They meditated on the effect of solar rays which do not stop at the surface of the body but penetrate the organism at the point where the solar plexus is located, bathing the body and the nervous system in the radiation of the Sun. This point is the oldest unity in the human organism.

The purpose of this Communion was to become receptive to the solar energies and establish a perfect unity between the self and the sun and distribute its power throughout the body.

By the Essenes' use of this method certain abnormal conditions were frequently cured in a way that seemed miraculous to the early historians.

The Angel of Water—Thursday Morning

The Essenes considered the circulation of water in nature to correspond to the circulation of the blood in the body. They knew all organisms as well as their foods consist largely of water, which is also essential to life on earth. The perfection of the organism depends upon the quality of the blood, and in like manner the perfection of the physical environment depends upon the quality of the water available.

In this Communion all forms of water were contemplated, rivers, creeks, rain, the sap in trees and plants and so on, establishing as a living reality the unity between the waters of the body and the waters of the planet, thereby making it possible to direct the blood stream to any part of the body or withdraw it at will.

This power enabled the Essenes to cure many conditions otherwise remedied only by long and arduous treatment. It was one of the reasons the Essenes had such complete self mastery and an almost unbelievable resistance to pain.

Angel of the Air—Friday Morning

The purpose of this Communion was to make man conscious of the dynamic unity between air and life and that respiration is the link between the organism and the cosmos, that where there is life there is breath, the cessation of one meaning the cessation of the other. Thus the atmosphere in surrounding nature and the air within the body have a stupendous role in health and vitality.

This Communion was accompanied by a certain deep rhythmic breathing enabling the Essenes to absorb specific energies from the atmosphere and establish a correlation of the self and the universe.

These Communions with the Earthly Mother and her Angels were the source from which the Essenes derived their particular way of living, their eating, cold water ablutions, sun bathing, breathing and so on, described by their contemporaries, Josephus, Philo and Pliny, with such astonishment.

THE EVENING COMMUNIONS

In the same way that the seven mornings of the week were devoted to the forces of the visible world, the seven evenings were given to the powers of the invisible realms, or the Angels of the Heavenly Father.

The Heavenly Father—Friday Evening

This Communion with the Heavenly Father, the Creator, the Light, the Ahura Mazda of Zoroaster, was the Essenes' central communion, dedicated to the totality of cosmic laws and to the realization that the universe is a process of continuous creation in which man must take his part by continuing the work of the Creator on earth.

The purpose of the Communion is to teach man the importance of union with the eternal and boundless cosmic ocean of all the superior radiations from all the planets, to make him receptive to these powers so that he may attain cosmic consciousness, enabling him to unite himself with the cosmic currents. Through this he can develop the creative abilities within him to the utmost and learn to use the creative principle in his life and surroundings.

The Essenes knew that only when man does this can he reach his final goal, union with the Heavenly Father, the ultimate aim of all Essenes and the underlying purpose governing all their actions, feelings and thoughts.

The Angel of Eternal Life—Saturday Evening

The Essenes considered that the purpose of the universe can only be eternal life, immortality; and that this can be achieved by man if he progressively creates the preconditions of his advance to higher and higher degrees of his individual evolution. They held that there was no limit to this progress since the cosmos is an inexhaustible store of energies available to man as he perfects his receptive organs and centers.

Through this Communion man can arouse his intuitive knowledge of the eternity of life in the universe and his own unity with this eternal life and the whole cosmic order. Through it he can learn the importance of overcoming gravity in the earthly currents of thought and become conscious of the superior currents' activity and role in the individual's and the planetary evolution.

This overcoming of gravity and absorbing and utilizing the superior currents from this and all other planets was the highest mystical accomplishment of the Essenes.

The Angel of Creative Work—Sunday Evening

This Communion was dedicated to all the great things which have been created by human labor, the great masterpieces of literature, art, science, philosophy and everything man has created as a superstructure on nature, the great values brought forth by previous generations and inherited by the present one.

The purpose of the Communion was to teach the importance of creative work and its paramount role in the individual's evolution. It was also to enable him to absorb energies and power from the creative works of mankind, all of its masterpieces, and to use this power in all manifestations of his consciousness.

In the Essene Brotherhoods everyone carried on creative work of some kind, whether in the improvement of himself, the Brotherhood or mankind. The Essenes considered creative work the most adequate expression of love.

The Angel of Peace—Monday Evening

The Communion with the Angel of Peace was dedicated to man's deep inner intuition of peace within himself and with all the infinite universe. In the Essene concept peace is one of the most valuable treasures of man and unless he realizes its true meaning he cannot have spirituality, without which his life can have no meaning. It was held that man's most immediate duty is to create peace within himself and with everything around him; and that the work of peace begins inside himself.

The Essenes utilized all sources of peace in the universe and transmitted them to the world, one manifestation of which was in their universal greeting, "Peace be with you."

The Angel of Power—Tuesday Evening

The Essenes conceived of the whole universe as a cosmic ocean of life in which currents of cosmic power are continually uniting all forms of life on all planets and connecting man with all other organisms.

The Communion made man conscious of these cosmo-vital forces surrounding him and within him. By becoming receptive to their activity he can absorb them through his nervous system and utilize them in every department of his life.

The Essenes were able to absorb and utilize these currents to a remarkable degree.

The Angel of Love—Wednesday Evening

Love was considered by the Essenes to be the highest creative feeling and they held that a cosmic ocean of love exists everywhere uniting all forms of life, and that life itself is an expression of love.

The purpose of the Communion is to teach man the importance and meaning of these superior currents of feeling in himself and in the surrounding universe; and to make him conscious of and receptive to them as a powerful source of energy and power which he can concentrate and direct in all manifestations of his consciousness.

In the concept of the Essenes, any individual who hurts any form of life outside himself hurts himself equally, because of the dynamic unity of all forms of life in the cosmic ocean of love. The Essenes themselves expressed strong feelings of love to the whole of mankind, near and far, and to all forms of life on earth and in infinite space.

This love which they felt was the cause of their living together in brotherhood communities; it was why they distributed all their surplus of food to the needy and went out of their way to teach the ignorant and heal the sick. They expressed their love through deeds.

This faculty of attracting and sending forth superior currents of feeling was one of their great mystical accomplishments.

The Angel of Wisdom—Thursday Evening

Thought was held by the Essenes to be both a cosmic and a cerebral function. They considered there is a cosmic ocean of thought pervading all space containing all thought, which is the highest and most powerful of all cosmic energies, never perishing and never lost.

By tuning in to all thought currents in the universe and the thought of all great thinkers of the past through communion with the Angel of Wisdom, man developed his ability to create powerful harmonious thought currents and attain intuitive knowledge and wisdom.

Through the application of this Communion the Essenes had great ability to send and receive powerful thought currents.

This Communion with the Angel of Wisdom completes the fourteen Communions of the Essenes. The morning Communions refer to the vitality of the body and their cumulative effect is the gradual strengthening and revitalizing of every organ of the body through the conscious control and direction of earthly forces.

The seven evening Communions are dedicated to the spiritual powers which govern man's higher evolution. Their cumulative effect is the revitalizing of the mind and all the superior forces within the individual, enabling him to receive and become attuned with all the higher oceans of love, life and thought, thus gradually developing all the superior potentialities of his being.

Each Communion of the fourteen represents a certain equilibrium between the man making it and the angel or force communed with.

THE NOON CONTEMPLATIONS

A third group of practices was held at noon each day of the week. These were contemplations calling upon the Heavenly Father to send His Angel of Peace to harmonize the different departments of man's life. So important was peace to the Essenes that they had a special teaching concerning it which they called the Sevenfold Peace.

The practice of the fourteen Communions brings about an inner experience or expansion of consciousness enabling the individual to make conscious use of the invisible forces of nature and the cosmos. The Sevenfold Peace shows the practical application of this expanded consciousness in the individual's daily life in its relationship to the different aspects of life.

These Peace Contemplations were practiced in the following order.

Friday noon—Peace with the Body.

Thursday noon—Peace with the Mind.

Wednesday noon—Peace with the Family.

Tuesday noon—Peace with Humanity.

Monday noon—Peace with Culture.

Sunday noon—Peace with the Earthly Mother.

Saturday noon—Peace with the Heavenly Father.

An explanation of these seven departments of the individual's life is given in a subsequent chapter.

Every seventh day, the Essene Sabbath, was consecrated to one of the aspects of peace and communal gatherings were held, separate from the individual contemplations. These gatherings were for the purpose of considering the practical collective application of the particular peace being concentrated upon on that Sabbath.

THE GREAT SABBATH

Every seventh Sabbath was called the Great Sabbath and was dedicated to Peace with the Heavenly Father. This was the transcendental Peace, containing all other aspects of peace. Thus every phase of man's life was given consideration, one after the other.

Such was the Essene pattern of Communion with the cosmic and natural forces and contemplation with the aspects of peace that showed them how to put the forces into practice in their individual lives. We shall not find its equivalent in any other system. It has the wisdom of eight thousand years behind it. It is not merely a form or a ritual; it is a dynamic, intuitive experience. It can establish the unity of mankind.

The Essenes practiced these Communions and Contemplations more than two thousand years ago. We can practice them today.

"I will praise Thy works
with songs of Thanksgiving
continually, from period to period,
in the circuits of the day, and in its fixed order;
with the coming of light from its source
and at the turn of evening and the outgoing of light,
at the outgoing of darkness and the coming in of day,
continually,
in all the generations of time."

From the "Thanksgiving Psalms"
of the Dead Sea Scrolls
XVII (xii. 4-12)

Chapter 5

The Essene Communions

II — THEIR ACTUAL PRACTICE

Fragmentary records of ancient traditions which have come down to us show that during eons of time man has gradually begun to develop within his being a certain receptive apparatus through which he is able to absorb the currents of force flowing in and around him, and consciously utilize them as sources of energy, harmony and knowledge.

The Essenes considered that the development of these receptive centers was an essential part of the individual's evolution. They also considered that systematic and daily practice of a correct method was necessary for the development of them.

The first part of their Communions taught the meaning and purpose of each of the fourteen terrestrial and cosmic forces. The second part was the actual practice or technique by which this apparatus can be developed.

Through this practice the subtle centers of the body can be opened and access given to the universal storehouse of cosmic forces. The purpose of this was to put the organs of the physical body in harmony with all beneficial currents of the earth and the cosmos, so that they can be utilized for the evolution of the individual and the planet.

Many early peoples had a similar technique. The Sumerians, the Persians at the time of Zoroaster, and the Hindus in their yoga systems, nine of which have survived the original fourteen, all sought to attain the same ends.

The technique which the Essenes handed down by word of mouth from generation to generation, through thousands of years, was given to the neophyte in their Brotherhoods only after seven years' probationary training had been completed. He then had to take the Great Sevenfold Vow, never to reveal the communions without permission, and never to use the knowledge and power gained through them for material or selfish purposes.

PROLOGUE TO THE COMMUNIONS

Previous to speaking the actual words of a communion, the Essene solemnly and reverently repeated the following prologue:

"I enter the Eternal and Infinite Garden with reverence to the Heavenly Father, the Earthly Mother and Great Masters, reverence to the holy, pure and saving Teaching, reverence to the Brotherhood of the Elect."

He then thought reverently about the angel or force with which he was about to commune, contemplating its meaning and purpose in his own life and body, as taught in the first part of the Communions.

Following this prologue he spoke the actual words of the Communion.

THE ACTUAL MORNING COMMUNIONS

1

To commune with the Earthly Mother, on Saturday morning, he says,

"The Earthly Mother and I are one.
She gives the food of Life to my whole body."

When he finishes these words he contemplates edible fruits, grains or plants and feels the currents of the Earthly Mother flowing in him and intensifying and directing the metabolism of his body.

2

On Sunday morning he communes with the Angel of Earth, saying:

"Angel of Earth, enter my generative organs
and regenerate my whole body."

As he says this he contemplates the life-generating soil and the growing grass, feeling the currents of the Angel of Earth transforming his sexual energy into regenerative forces.

On Monday morning he communes with the Angel of Life in the following words:
"Angel of Life, enter my limbs
and give strength to my whole body."
He now contemplates trees as he feels himself absorbing vital forces from trees and forests.

The words of the Tuesday morning Communion with the Angel of Joy are:
"Angel of Joy, descend upon earth
and give beauty to all beings."
He then feels himself absorbing vibrations of joy from the beauties of nature as he contemplates the colors of sunrise, of sunset, the song of a bird or the aroma of a flower.

The Wednesday morning Communion to the Angel of the Sun uses these words:
"Angel of Sun, enter my Solar Center
and give the fire of life to my whole body."
As these words are spoken he contemplates the rising sun and feels and directs the accumulated solar forces radiating through his solar center, located at the solar plexus, sending them to all parts of his body.

6

The Thursday morning Communion with the Angel of Water is made by saying:
"Angel of Water, enter my blood
and give the water of Life to my whole body."
As he says this he contemplates the waters of the earth, in rain, river, lake, sea or anywhere, and the currents of the Angel of Water are felt intensifying and directing the circulation of the blood.

At the Communion on Friday morning with the Angel of Air, the Essene says:
"Angel of Air, enter my lungs
and give the air of Life to my whole body."
The one communing contemplates the atmosphere as he says this and breathes rhythmically.

THE ACTUAL EVENING COMMUNIONS

The words of the evening Communions with the Heavenly Father and his Angels follow.

1

The Friday evening Communion with the Heavenly Father begins by saying:
> "The Heavenly Father and I are One."

This Communion in time brings union with the eternal and boundless cosmic ocean of all superior radiations from all planets, as cosmic consciousness is awakened and the individual is finally united with the Supreme Power.

2

The Saturday evening Communion with the Angel of Eternal Life declares:
> "Angel of Eternal Life, descend upon me
> and give Eternal Life to my spirit."

As these words are said the individual contemplates union with the currents of thought of the superior planets and gains power to overcome the sphere of gravitation of earthly currents of thought.

3

On Sunday evening the Communion with the Angel of Creative Work gives this command:
> "Angel of Creative Work, descend upon humanity
> and give abundance to all men."

The contemplation is upon bees at work, and the creative work of humanity in all spheres of existence is concentrated upon.

4

The Communion on Monday evening with the Angel of Peace is made with these words:
> "Peace, peace, peace,
> Angel of Peace,
> Be always everywhere."

The individual now contemplates the crescent moon and the moonlight, invoking and visualizing universal peace in all spheres of existence.

The Tuesday evening Communion with the Angel of Power says:

"Angel of Power, descend upon my Acting Body
and direct all my acts."

As he contemplates the stars, their radiations, and the cosmic ocean of Life, the individual feels the cosmo-vital forces from the stars being absorbed by the nervous system of the Acting Body.

6

The Wednesday evening Communion is with the Angel of Love. These are the words spoken:

"Angel of Love, descend upon my Feeling Body
and purify all my feelings."

While this is being said the Feeling Body both sends and attracts superior currents of feeling to and from all beings on earth and all those in the cosmic ocean of Love.

7

Thursday evening is dedicated to the Angel of Wisdom who is addressed as follows:

"Angel of Wisdom, descend upon my Thinking
Body and enlighten all my thoughts."

Superior currents of thought are then sent and attracted by the Thinking Body while the individual contemplates all thought on earth and in the cosmic ocean of thought.

These are the traditional words of the Communions with the Earthly Mother and the Heavenly Father and their Angels. The cumulative effect of the regular weekly repetition of each of these Communions enables the individual, sooner or later, according to his capacity, perseverence and the degree of his evolution, to absorb, utilize and direct these currents of energy in all manifestations of his consciousness, for his own higher evolution and that of mankind and the planet.

THE ACTUAL NOON CONTEMPLATIONS

The Noon Peace Contemplations, dedicated each day to a different one of the seven aspects of Peace, were addressed to the Heavenly Father, requesting him to send the Angel of Peace to all, and then to send a certain one of the angels to strengthen each aspect of the Sevenfold Peace. The words follow:

Friday noon (Peace With the Body):

> Our Father who art in heaven,
> send to all
> your Angel of Peace;
> to our body
> the Angel of Life.

Thursday noon (Peace With the Mind):

> Our Father who art in heaven,
> send to all
> your Angel of Peace;
> to our mind
> the Angel of Power.

Wednesday noon: (Peace With the Family):

> Our Father who are in heaven,
> send to all
> Your Angel of Peace;
> to our family and friends
> the Angel of Love.

Tuesday noon (Peace With Humanity):

> Our Father who art in heaven,
> send to all
> Your Angel of Peace;
> to humanity
> the Angel of Work.

Monday noon (Peace With Culture):

> Our Father who art in heaven,
> send to all
> Your Angel of Peace;
> to our knowledge,
> the Angel of Wisdom.

**Sunday noon (Peace With the Kingdom of
The Earthly Mother):**

> Our Father who art in heaven,
> send to all
> Your Angel of Peace;
> to the kingdom of our Earthly Mother,
> the Angel of Joy.

**Saturday noon (Peace With the Kingdom of
The Heavenly Father):**

> Our Father who art in heaven,
> send to all
> Your Angel of Peace;
> to Your Kingdom, our Heavenly Father,
> Your Angel of Eternal Life.

	MORNING COMMUNIONS		
		Contemplative	Force
Sat.	Earthly Mother	Food	Nutrition
Sun.	Angel of Earth	Top Soil Growth	Regeneration Glands
Mon.	Angel of Life	Trees	Vitality Life Force
Tues.	Angel of Joy	Beauty	Harmony
Wed.	Angel of Sun	Sunrise	Fire of Life
Thurs.	Angel of Water	Blood Rivers etc.	Circulation
Fri.	Angel of Air	Breath	Energies of Atmosphere

The Communions

with the Forces of the Visible Realms

	NOON CONTEMPLATIONS
	Peace with the
Saturday	Kingdom of the Heavenly Father
Sunday	Kingdom of the Earthly Mother
Monday	Culture
Tuesday	Humanity (Social Peace)
Wednesday	Family (Feeling Body)
Thursday	Mind (Thinking Body)
Friday	Body (Acting Body)

The Noon

Peace Contemplations

	EVENING COMMUNIONS		
		Contemplative	Force
Sat.	Angel of Eternal Life	Superior Planets	Overcoming Gravity
Sun.	Angel of Creative Work	Bees	Creative Work of Man
Mon.	Angel of Peace	Crescent Moon	Peace Within
Tues.	Angel of Power	Stars Superior Acts	Nervous System Cosmic Ocean of Life
Wed.	Angel of Love	Superior Feeling	Emotions Cosmic Ocean of Love
Thurs.	Angel of Wisdom	Superior Thoughts	Thinking Body
Fri.	Heavenly Father	Cosmic Currents	Final Union with Cosmic Ocean

The Communions

with the Powers of the Invisible Realms

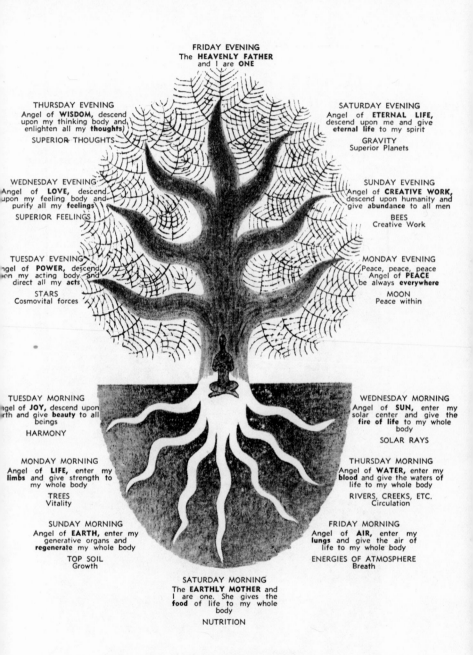

FRIDAY EVENING
The **HEAVENLY FATHER**
and I are **ONE**

THURSDAY EVENING
Angel of **WISDOM**, descend
upon my thinking body and
enlighten all my **thoughts**
SUPERIOR THOUGHTS

SATURDAY EVENING
Angel of **ETERNAL LIFE**,
descend upon me and give
eternal life to my spirit
GRAVITY
Superior Planets

WEDNESDAY EVENING
Angel of **LOVE**, descend
upon my feeling body and
purify all my **feelings**
SUPERIOR FEELINGS

SUNDAY EVENING
Angel of **CREATIVE WORK**,
descend upon humanity and
give **abundance** to all men
BEES
Creative Work

TUESDAY EVENING
Angel of **POWER**, descend
upon my acting body and
direct all my **acts**
STARS
Cosmovital forces

MONDAY EVENING
Peace, peace, peace
Angel of **PEACE**
be always **everywhere**
MOON
Peace within

TUESDAY MORNING
Angel of **JOY**, descend upon
earth and give **beauty** to all
beings
HARMONY

WEDNESDAY MORNING
Angel of **SUN**, enter my
solar center and give the
fire of life to my whole
body
SOLAR RAYS

MONDAY MORNING
Angel of **LIFE**, enter my
limbs and give strength to
my whole body
TREES
Vitality

THURSDAY MORNING
Angel of **WATER**, enter my
blood and give the waters of
life to my whole body
RIVERS, CREEKS, ETC.
Circulation

SUNDAY MORNING
Angel of **EARTH**, enter my
generative organs and
regenerate my whole body
TOP SOIL
Growth

FRIDAY MORNING
Angel of **AIR**, enter my
lungs and give the air of
life to my whole body
ENERGIES OF ATMOSPHERE
Breath

SATURDAY MORNING
The **EARTHLY MOTHER** and
I are one. She gives the
food of life to my whole
body
NUTRITION

THE ESSENE TREE OF LIFE
with the Morning and Evening Communions

"May He bless thee with every good,
may He keep thee from all evil
and illumine thy heart with the knowledge of life
and favor thee with eternal wisdom.
And may He give His Sevenfold blessings upon thee
to everlasting Peace."

From "The Manual of Discipline'
of the Dead Sea Scrolls

Chapter 6

The Sevenfold Peace

The Sevenfold Peace of the Essenes was the summation of their inner teaching.

Their Tree of Life and the Communions taught man his relationship with the fourteen forces of the visible and invisible worlds. The Sevenfold Peace explains his relationship to the parts of his own being and to his fellow men, showing how to create peace and harmony in the seven categories of his life.

Harmony to the Essenes meant peace.

They considered that human life can be divided into seven departments, physical, mental, emotional, social, cultural, its relationship with nature and its relationship with the entire cosmos.

Man, it was held, has three bodies that function in each of these departments, an acting body, a feeling body and a thinking body. The thinking body's highest power is wisdom. The feeling body's highest power is love. The acting body's function is to translate the wisdom of the thinking body and the love of the feeling body into action in an individual's social and cultural worlds and in his utilization of the terrestrial and heavenly forces.

The Sevenfold Peace explains the utilization of these powers and forces with the utmost clarity. Every noon a Peace Contemplation was held with one aspect of Peace; and every Sabbath was collectively dedicated to one, the entire cycle covering all phases of man's life being completed in seven weeks' time.

I — Peace With the Body

The word used by the Essenes to indicate the physical body, both in Aramaic and in Hebrew, signified the body's function, to act, to move.

This differs greatly from other concepts. The Greeks, for instance, exalted the body for its esthetic qualities, its proportions and beauty, and were unaware of any deeper purpose. The Romans looked upon the body simply as an instrument of strength and power for conquering nations, planting the Roman eagle in far lands. The medieval Christians disdained the body, considering it the source of all man's troubles, a barrier between man and God.

The Essenes had a much deeper understanding than any of these. They knew that in the acting body, evolving through hundreds of thousands of years, are manifested all the laws of life and the cosmos; in it is to be found the key to the whole universe.

They studied it in relation to man's whole role in the universe, and their concept of that role was greater than any other which has ever been held. They considered man has three roles: one of individual evolution; second, a function in regard to the planet on which he lives; and third, a purpose as a unit of the cosmos.

The acting body has its part to play in all three of these roles. It is a Divine product, created by the law for the purpose of the Creator, in no way inferior to any other instrument of man, nor to anything else in the universe. It is waiting for man to make conscious use of its terrestrial and spiritual energies.

The Essenes knew that man is not an isolated being alone in the universe, but one among other beings on earth and on other planets, all of whom have acting bodies which are evolving even as is man's own. All of these acting bodies are therefore related to each other and affect each other. Every individual's bodily health and vitality is consequently of the utmost importance both to himself and to all other beings on earth and on all other planets.

The daily practices of the Essenes were derived from this dynamic all-sided concept of the acting body as an integral part of the whole universe and their extraordinary health and vitality was a result of it.

Those who joined their Brotherhoods were trained to perfect the acting body in all three of its roles, and were taught how to adapt it to the constantly changing field of forces in which it lives and moves.

They were taught the effects on the organism of different foods and the different natural forces of earth, the sun, air and water. They were required to follow certain rituals utilizing these forces, such as starting each day with a cold water ablution and exposing the body once every day to the solar rays. Through practical experience they learned the vitalizing power of working in the fields and orchards and gardens.

They learned how disease is created by deviations from the law and how to heal the diseases that result from the deviations. They were taught the qualities and curative powers of different herbs and plants, of heliotherapy and hydrotherapy, and the proper diet for every ailment. They were instructed in right breathing and in the power which thought holds over the acting body.

They learned the material and spiritual value of moderation in all things, and that fasting was a way to regenerate the body and to develop the will and in this way to increase spiritual power.

These practices brought peace and harmony to the acting body. But undue importance was never attached to it. The consideration and care they gave it was solely to keep it in good health as an instrument through which they could perform acts of wisdom and love for their fellowman. In this way the acting body participated in the evolution of the individual, of the planet and the cosmos, thus enabling the individual to become a co-creator with the law and with God.

This was the first peace practiced by the Essenes, peace with the body.

II — Peace With the Mind

The quintessence of the teaching in the Sevenfold Peace was concentrated around peace with the mind, mind, in the Essene terminology, being the creator of thought.

The Essenes considered thought to be a superior force, more powerful than the force of either feeling or action, because it is the instigator of both.

The totality of an individual's thoughts was called his thinking body. The totality of the thoughts in all the hundreds of millions of thinking bodies around the surface of the earth forms the planetary thinking body; and the totality of all superior thoughts in the universe forms a cosmic thinking body, or a cosmic ocean of thought.

The Essenes considered an individual's thinking body, like his acting body, has three functions, an individual, a planetary and a cosmic function.

It's individual function is to utilize the power of thought to guide and direct the currents of feeling in the individual's feeling body, and the actions of his acting body. The thinking body can do this because it penetrates through and though the feeling and acting bodies.

The planetary function is to contribute noble and uplifting thoughts to the planetary thinking body. An individual's thoughts form a force field around him comparable to the magnetic field surrounding a magnetic pole. Into this force field the individual's thoughts are constantly pouring and being sent out, and it is also receiving currents of thought from the planetary thinking body of which it is a part. Every individual thus lives, moves, thinks, feels and acts in this surrounding planetary atmosphere of thought, to which he himself is constantly contributing. He is responsible for the thoughts he contributes, for all the thoughts he sends out.

The third function of the thinking body, its cosmic function, is not readily fulfilled. The cosmic ocean of thought, of which the planetary thought atmosphere surrounding the earth is only an infinitesimal part, consists of all the thoughts in the universe superior enough to have become freed of the planetary forces attaching them to their particular planet. Only those highest thought currents which have overcome the planetary gravitation of their planetary atmosphere become united with the infinite cosmic ocean of thought.

This cosmic ocean of thought represents the perfection of the law, the omnipotence of the law and the omnipresence of the law. It has always existed and it always will exist. It is more ancient than any of the existing planets in the solar system, more ancient than the existing solar system itself, or than the galactic or ultra-galactic systems. Eternal and infinite it directs all the steps of the cosmic and planetary evolution in the infinite cosmic ocean of life.

The cosmic function of each individual's thinking body is to create thoughts of so superior a quality that they can unite with this cosmic ocean of thought.

The Essenes considered that the thinking body is man's highest gift from his Creator. For it, and it alone, gives him the capacity to become conscious of the Law, to understand it, to work in harmony with it, to perceive its manifestations in all his surroundings, in himself, in every cell and molecule of his physical body, in everything that is, and to realize its omnipresence and omnipotence. By becoming conscious of the Law, by understanding it, by acting in harmony with it, man becomes a co-creator with God; there is no greater or higher value in the universe.

Through this most powerful force of thought, this greatest of treasures possessed by man, and his title to nobility, man has the ability and freedom to accomplish whatever he truly wants, to achieve anything to which he aspires that is in harmony with the Law, and thereby to live in the eternal perfection that is the Law.

If man thinks in harmony with the Law he can remedy whatever inharmony he has created in the past; he can recreate his thinking body, his feeling body and his acting body. He can heal all diseases in his physical body and create complete harmony in his environment and world.

But if the currents of thought in the thinking body are not in accord with the Law, nothing else can create harmony in the individual's world.

The Essenes knew that only a small minority of mankind make use of the great capacity of the thinking body. They knew that the majority use their thinking bodies quite haphazardly, unaware their thoughts can be used to build or to destroy. An almost automatic succession of thoughts, ideas and association of ideas passes through their minds without conscious direction. Yet even these drifting elements of thought can create powerful forces that go through and through the feeling body and the acting body, interpenetrating every atom and cell, throwing every particle of them into vibration. From these vibrations radiations go out that are harmonious or inharmonious according to the nature of the thought.

If man fails to become consciously aware of the Law, he deviates from it unknowingly for he is surrounded by fields of inharmonious forces prompting him to deviations. These deviations create all the imperfections in his world, all the limitations and negations in his thoughts and feelings and physical well-being, in his environment, in society and the entire planet. Every time man creates or accepts an inferior thought, he is accepting an inferior force into his world.

The inferior force, according to the strength of the thought, reacts on his feeling body. This sets up an emotional disequilibrium in his feeling body, which in turn reacts on his physical body.

This disequilibrium automatically causes further deviations, further inharmonies, further diseases in the feeling and acting bodies. And these inharmonies, these diseases, create an inharmonious atmosphere around the individual which affects the thinking, feeling and acting bodies of all others who are not conscious of the Law and do not know how to protect themselves from receiving all those inferior thoughts created by the individual's single deviation in thought.

So every individual who has an inferior thought, a limiting, negative or inharmonious thought, starts a chain reaction of deviations which spreads throughout the planet and the planetary worlds, causing even further deviations, negations, limitations and inharmonies.

This inharmony is contagious just as many diseases are contagious. But the great Essene masters taught man how to prevent these waves of inharmony, right at their source, before the first inharmonious thought is created. They taught man the right way of thinking, the way of never deviating from the Law, never receiving or accepting into the consciousness any thought less than perfection.

These great masters also taught that man is free to work with the Law if he so desires, creating ever increasing harmony and perfection in his world and in the world outside of himself.

Man continually tries to evolve ways to better the conditions in which he lives. But he does this too often without regard for the Law. He seeks peace and harmony by material means, technical evolution, economic systems, not knowing that the conditions of inharmony which he himself has brought into being can never be remedied by material means. The ocean of suffering and inharmony humanity has created can only be destroyed when mankind sets into motion the law of harmony in his thinking body. Only through complete cooperation with the Law can peace and harmony be brought to the planet.

This is the teaching of the ancient Essenes in regard to peace with the mind.

III — Peace With the Family

The third peace of the Essenes, peace with the family, concerns harmony in the feeling body, harmony in the emotions.

By the term family the Essenes meant those in the individual's immediate environment, the people he contacts in his daily life and thought, his family, relatives, friends and associates. According to the Essene tradition harmony with these people depends upon the feeling body.

The natural function of the feeling body is to express love. Mankind has been told this over and over again by the great Masters, Jesus, Buddha, Zoroaster, Moses and the Prophets. He has been given the law that he should love his Creator with all his thinking, feeling and acting bodies. Life in all its spheres, aspects and manifestations is the demonstration of creative love.

Divine love is a great cosmic power, a cosmic function. It is the law of all man's bodies, but it is expressed most powerfully through the feeling body.

The feeling body consists of all the currents of feeling and emotions an individual experiences and sends out into the atmosphere about him.

Just as the thinking bodies of all the individuals on the planet create a thought atmosphere around it, so all the feeling bodies create a planetary feeling atmosphere, invisible and imponderable, but having enormous influence and power. Every feeling and emotion created by an individual becomes a part of the feeling atmosphere of earth, setting up a resonance of co-vibration with all similar feelings in the earth's atmosphere.

If an inferior feeling is sent out, its creator is immediately tuned in to all the similar inferior feelings in the earth's feeling body. He thus opens the gate to a flood of destructive power which rushes in and seizes control of his feelings, and often of his mind, amplifying his own low feelings just as a loud speaker amplifies or intensifies sound.

This destructive force directly affects the individual's physical body. It affects the functioning of the endocrine glands and the whole glandular system. It produces disease cells that lower vitality, shorten life and result in unlimited suffering. It is thus not surprising that statistics of nervous disorders and other diseases are so appalling in spite of all the hospitals, sanitariums, medical organizations, laboratories and the progress of hygiene and medicine.

Through his feeling body man has become an auto-intoxicating automaton, because of his deviation from the law, his acting without knowledge of the law, against it instead of with it.

The Essenes knew that there is a great deal of inharmony in the feeling body of almost everyone. By studying the feeling bodies of babies and primitive man they learned why.

The feeling body of a baby first registers the manisfestations of the infant's primitive instinct of self-preservation. This instinct arouses three fundamental emotions: fear, anger and love. Fear arises from a sudden movement or noise; anger from interference with the baby's freedom; love from the satisfaction of its hunger and needs. Fear and anger are inferior feelings; the love feeling, while superior, in the baby is rudimentary. The baby's feeling body is a volcano of emotions, most of which are inferior. Its thinking body has not begun to function.

A primitive man has a similar feeling body. His emotions, likewise centered around the instinct of self-preservation, are a powerful force completely dominating his embryonic thinking body.

In both child and primitive man the feeling body

develops long before the thinking body. This is necessary to protect the physical body from danger and so preserve its life. The instinct of self-preservation is a law of nature. Acting under it is in entire harmony with the law until man has evolved the power to think and reason his way out of danger.

But because feeling has functioned for so much longer a period of time than thinking, it tends to dominate thought even after the child is grown and the primitive man has become civilized. In the mass of mankind today the feeling body rules the thinking body.

This is the cause of man's first deviation from the law.

Through the power of thought man can handle every situation in his life more adequately than through unthinking emotion. But the actions of most people are far more often the expression of impulses in the feeling body than of reasoned thought. This results in a tremendous imbalance in his bodies. Because adult civilized man has evolved to the point where he has the ability to think, thought should govern his actions. When he permits them to be controlled by emotion and feeling, as they were dominated in infancy, he throws all his powers out of rhythm, out of harmony.

This creates a regressive psychological condition in his whole existence. His deeds and actions as a consequence remain self-centered and egoistic like those of a child or primitive man. But when he is no longer a savage or a child, he deviates from the law if he acts as a child or primitive man. His instinctive impulses can only serve evolutionary progress when controlled by the thinking faculties.

There are further consequences from this deviation from the law.

Nature has given man the capacity to think so he may be able to understand its laws and direct his life in harmony with them. Man can reach a far higher degree of evolution through thinking than through living by instinct. So when he continues to let his feeling body be the dominating power in his actions, he not only retards his own evolution but that of the planet.

If he makes no effort to understand the law but neglects it and consequently lacks knowledge of it, he has to create his own laws, small artificial laws, of self-centeredness and egoism; and these cause walls of separation between himself and the rest of the human family, between himself and nature and between himself and the Great Law, the Creator.

Man's first deviation from the law through the feeling body starts the long chain of deviations which cause all human inharmony and suffering on earth.

All the great teachers of humanity through thousands of years have warned man of the consequences of deviation from the law of the feeling body. Buddha pointed out how it results in suffering, suffering for the individual and suffering for humanity.

The Essenes showed that the feeling body can be the most powerful instrument for the production of health, vitality and happiness, and that through its right functioning in expressing love, man can create the kingdom of heaven in and around himself and the whole human family.

The Essene peace with the family is the Great Law in its expression of men's love toward one another, a law revealed to little children but often hidden from the minds of men.

IV — Peace With Humanity

The fourth peace of the Essenes referred to harmony between groups of people, to social and economic peace.

Mankind has never enjoyed social peace in any age in history. Man has always exploited man economically, oppressed him politically, suppressed him by military force. The Essenes knew these injustices were caused by deviations from the law. The very same deviations that produce inharmony in man's personal life, in his acting, thinking and feeling bodies, produce wealth and poverty, masters and slaves, social unrest.

The Essenes regarded both riches and poverty to be the result of deviations from the law.

Great wealth, they considered, is concentrated into the hands of the few because of man's exploitation of man, in one way or another. This has caused misery for both suppressor and suppressed. The many feel hatred and its kindred destructive emotions. This produces fear in the hearts of the exploiters, fear of revolt, fear of losing their possessions, even their lives.

Poverty was held to be an equal deviation from the law. A man is poor because of wrong attitudes of thinking, feeling and acting. He is ignorant of the law and fails to work with the law. The Essenes showed that there is an abundance for everyone of all that a man needs for his use and happiness.

Limitations and over-abundance are both artificial states, deviations from the law. They produce the vicious circle of fear and revolt, a permanent atmosphere of inharmony, affecting the thinking, feeling and acting bodies of both rich and poor, continually creating a state of unrest, war and chaos. This has been the condition throughout recorded history.

The rich and the poor alike suffer the consequences of their deviations.

The Essenes knew there was no escape from this circle of oppression, hatreds and violence, wars and revolutions, except through changing the ignorance of the individuals in the world. They knew it takes a long time for an individual to change his ideas, thinking and habits and learn to cooperate with the law. The individual himself has to do the changing; nobody else can do it for him.

But a higher and higher understanding of the law can be brought about gradually, the Essenes believed, through teaching and example. They taught a quite opposite way of existence from either poverty or great wealth. They demonstrated in their daily lives that if man lives according to the law, seeks to understand the law and consciously cooperates with it, he will know no lack. He will be able to maintain an all-sided harmony in every act and thought and feeling, and he will find his every need fulfilled.

The solution which the Essenes offered for economic and social harmony can be applied in every age, the present as well as the past. It contained four factors:

1. Separating from the chaotic conditions of the mass of mankind which refuses to obey natural and cosmic law.

2. Demonstrating a practical social system based on natural and cosmic law.

3. Communicating these ideas to the outside world through teaching, healing and helping others according to their needs.

4. Attracting to their communities other individuals who are sufficiently evolved to be willing to cooperate with the law.

The Essenes withdrew from the inharmony of cities and towns and formed brotherhoods on the shores of lakes and rivers where they could live and work in obedience to the law. They established there economic and social systems based wholly on the law. No rich and no poor were in their brotherhoods. No one had need of anything he did not have; and no one had an excess of things he could not use. They considered one condition as deteriorating as the other.

They demonstrated to humanity that man's daily bread, his food and all his material needs can be acquired without struggle through the knowledge of the law.

Strict rules and regulations were unnecessary for all lived in accord with the law. Order, efficiency and individual freedom existed side by side. The Essenes were extremely practical as well as highly spiritual and intellectual.

They took no part in politics and adhered to no political factions, knowing that neither political or military means could change man's chaotic condition. They showed by concrete example that exploitation and oppression of others were completely unnecessary. Many economic and social historians have considered the Essenes the world's first social reformers on a comprehensive scale.

Their brotherhoods were partly cooperative. Each member of the group had his own small house and a garden large enough for him to grow whatever he especially desired. But he also took part in communal activities wherever his service might be needed, such as in the pasturing of animals, planting and harvesting of crops most economically grown on an extensive basis.

They had great agricultural proficiency, a thorough

knowledge of plant life, soil and climatic conditions. In comparatively desert areas they produced a large variety of fruits and vegetables of the highest quality and in such abundance they periodically had a surplus to distribute to the needy. Their scientific knowledge was such that they could do all of this in a comparatively few hours each day, leaving ample time for their studies and spiritual practices.

Nature was their Bible. They considered gardening educational, a key to the understanding of the entire universe, revealing all its laws, even as does the acting body. They read and studied the great book of nature throughout their lives, in all their brotherhoods, as an inexhaustible source of knowledge, as well as of energy and harmony. When they dug in their gardens and tended their plantings they held communion with the growing things, the trees, sun, soil, rain. From all of these forces they received their education, their pleasure and their recreation.

One of the reasons for their great success was this attitude toward their work. They did not consider it as work but as a means of studying the forces and laws of nature. It was in this that their economic system differed from all others. The vegetables and fruits they produced were only the incidental results of their activities; their real reward was in the knowledge, harmony and vitality they gained to enrich their lives. Gardening was a ritual with them; a great and impressive silence reigned as they worked in harmony with nature creating veritable kingdoms of heaven in their brotherhoods.

Their economic and social organization was only one phase of their whole system of life and teaching. It was considered a means to an end, not an end in itself. There was thus a dynamic unity and harmony in all their activity, their thoughts and feelings and deeds. All gave freely of their time and energy with no mathematical measuring of one another's contributions. Through this harmony within each individual, the individual's evolution progressed steadily.

The Essenes knew it takes many generations to effect changes in people or in mankind as a whole, but they sent out teachers and healers from their brotherhoods whose lives and accomplishments would manifest the truths they taught and little by little increase mankind's understanding and desire to live in accord with the law. The Essene Brotherhood at the Dead Sea for many centuries sent out such teachers as John the Baptist, Jesus and John the Beloved. They warned again and again of the consequences of man's social and economic deviations from the law. Prophet after prophet was sent forth to warn of the dangers incurred by the social injustices that existed then even as they exist today. Not only were individuals and groups warned but it was shown that all who aided or in any way collaborated with the deviators were also in danger.

The mass of mankind failed to listen, failed to gain any understanding of social and economic peace. Only the few more evolved individuals heeded. Of these some were selected to work in the brotherhoods as examples of peace and harmony in all aspects of existence.

The Essenes knew that through the cumulative effect of example and teaching the minority who understand and obey the law will someday grow through the generations to become, finally, the majority of mankind.

Then and then only will mankind know this fourth peace of the Essenes, peace with humanity.

V — Peace With Culture

Peace with culture refers to the utilization of the masterpieces of wisdom from all ages, including the present.

The Essenes held that man can take his rightful place in the universe only by absorbing all possible knowledge from the great teachings which have been given forth by masters of wisdom.

According to the Essene traditions these masterpieces represented one-third of all knowledge. They considered there are three pathways to the finding of truth. One is the path of intuition which was followed by the mystics and prophets. Another is the pathway of nature, that of the scientist. The third is the pathway of culture, that of great masterpieces of literature and the arts.

The Essenes preserved many precious manuscripts in their brotherhoods which they constantly studied by a method found in no other school of thought in antiquity. They studied them by following the first two pathways to truth: intuition and nature.

Through intuition they endeavored to apprehend the original higher intuition of the master and so awaken their own higher consciousness. Through nature, from which the great masters drew comparisons to express their intuitive knowledge to the masses, the Essenes correlated their own intuitive observations with the teachings of the masters. By this continual comparison between nature, their own intuitions and the great masterpieces of culture, their own individual evolution was advanced.

It was also considered to be every man's duty to acquire the wisdom from these masterpieces so that the experience, knowledge and wisdom already attained by previous generations could be utilized. Without these teachings the progress and evolution of mankind would be much slower than it is, for every generation would have to start all over again from the beginning. In universal culture man has added something new to the planet and so has become a creator, a co-creator with God. Thus he performs his function on the planet by continuing the work of creation.

Universal culture is of great value to humanity from two other standpoints. First, it represents the highest ideals which mankind has held. Second, it represents an all-sided synthesis of knowledge of the problems of life and their right solution.

This knowledge was brought forth by highly evolved individuals, masters who had the power to contact the universal sources of knowledge, energy and harmony which exist in the cosmic ocean of thought. Evidence of this contact was their conscious directing of the forces of nature in ways the world today terms miracles. These manifestations of their powers drew about them a limited number of followers who were advanced enough in their own evolution to understand the deeper meaning of the master's teaching. These disciples endeavored to preserve the truths taught by writing down the master's words. This was the origin of all the great masterpieces of universal literature.

The truths in these masterpieces are eternal. They are valid for all time. They come from the one eternal unchanging source of all knowledge. The cosmic and natural laws, nature, man's inner consciousness are the same today as two or ten thousand years ago. Such teachings belong to no one school of thought or religion. The Essenes believed man should study all the great sacred books of humanity, all the great contributions to culture, for they knew all teach the same ageless wisdom and any seeming contradictions come through the one-sidedness of the followers who have attempted to interpret them.

The object of study, they held, is not to add a few additional facts to the store of knowledge an individual already may have. It is to open to him sources of universal truth. They considered that when a man reads a great sacred book of humanity, the symbols of letters and words themselves create in the thinking body powerful vibrations and currents of thought. These vibrations and currents put the individual in touch with the thinking body of the great master who gave forth the truth.

This opens up for the individual a source of knowledge, harmony and power obtainable in no other way. This is the great value, the inner meaning, of the fifth peace of the Essenes.

These great masterpieces have been brought forth in periods of history when humanity was in great chaos. Mankind's constant deviations from the law seem to culminate at certain times in mass confusion and disruption, threatening or completely bringing about the disintegration of the existing social order and way of life. At such periods the great masters have appeared as way showers to the people. Masters such as Zoroaster, Buddha, Moses, Jesus, brought new horizons and new hope to humanity.

They gave forth their teachings in two forms. One was in parables from nature which could be understood by the masses of the people. The other, given to the small minority of evolved followers, was transmitted direct from the master's consciousness to the consciousness of the disciple. The former are called the exoteric books and were referred to by historians as the written traditions. The other teaching was termed the unwritten tradition, and these were the esoteric teaching written down by the disciples for themselves, not for the people. But even the disciples did not always understand the master's wisdom and interpret it correctly.

A few, although only a very few, contemporary books contain the same teachings which the masters gave forth. Thousands of people write books today and thousands upon thousands of books are published each year. With such a mass production of printed matter it is inevitable that the vast majority of it must be of an inferior quality even the best of which proclaims shallow pseudo-truths. Yet what little time modern man allots to reading tends to be spent on this ephemeral and generaliy worthless printed matter, while the masterpieces of the ages gather dust on the library shelves.

Before printing was invented only those manuscripts which had real value were ever preserved. Only extraordinary books were produced. The average man was not able to read or write. The difficulties of acquiring knowledge were enormous. Traveling to the few centers of learning entailed great danger due to unsettled conditions in various countries and the primitive methods of transportation. The student moreover had to serve years of apprenticeship to be considered worthy of acquiring wisdom, and further long years in acquiring it. The material difficulties in producing a manuscript were also great. Because of these obstacles only works of true genius were transmitted to future generations and the few that have survived represent wisdom of the highest order.

This third part of all wisdom, represented by the culture of humanity, was held by the Essenes to be necessary for man's evolution. In no other way could he gain an all-sided understanding of the laws of life through contact with the cosmic ocean of thought.

This contact, through the eternal thinking body of a great master, is the sacred purpose and the priceless privilege of peace and harmony with culture.

VI — Peace With the Kingdom of the Earthly Mother

The sixth peace teaches harmony with the laws of terrestrial nature, the kingdom of the Earthly Mother. The unity of man and nature is a basic principle of the Essene science of life.

Man is an integral part of nature. He is governed by all the laws and forces of nature. His health, vitality and well-being depend upon his degree of harmony with earth forces; and that of every individual, every nation and the whole of humanity will always be in direct proportion to man's observance of terrestrial laws.

Universal history shows that every nation reached its greatest splendor by following the great law of unity between man and nature. Its vitality and prosperity flourished when the people lived a simple natural life of cooperation with nature. But when the nation or civilization deviates from unity, it inevitably disintegrates and disappears.

This unity of man and nature has never been so heavily transgressed as in the present day. Modern man's building of cities is in entire variance with nature. The city's stone and concrete walls are the symbols of man's separation from nature, of his aggressive way of life with its urges to subjugation of others and to constant competition, one with another. His present centralized, technical and mechanized life creates a chasm separating him from nature, a chasm which never was wider or deeper.

Unity with nature is the foundation of man's existence on the planet. It is the foundation of all economic systems, of all social relationships between groups of people. Without it, the present civilization like those of the past will move toward decline and decay.

This law of unity was held by the Essenes to be the guiding norm for the daily life of man in the material universe.

Humanity has had knowledge of this great law from a time preceding the Pleistocene cataclysm. According to traditions based on the hieroglyphics of the Sumerians made some ten thousand years ago the life of antediluvian man was preponderantly a forest life, inseparable from that of the forest. Science has named this man homo sapiens sylvanus.

The giant trees of that age, several hundred feet in height, not only provided shelter but regulated the temperature and humidity of the atmosphere. Trees produced man's food with an abundance of different fruits. Man's basic occupation was with trees. He not only cultivated and cared for them, he created new varieties producing new kinds of fruits. He was a great arboriculturist, living in harmony with all the forces of nature. He collaborated with her in every way, both extending the forests and abstaining from harming trees.

This antediluvian man of the forest ages, without technical development of any kind, was an almost perfect demonstration of the great law of unity and harmony between man and nature. In the philosophy of all ancient teachings man's unity with the forests was a basic characteristic. The idea of unity between man and nature has inspired great thinkers, philosophers and whole systems of thought.

Zoroaster based much of his teaching in the Zend Avesta upon it. He sought to renew the earlier traditions by leading man back into this harmonious way of life, collaboration with terrestrial nature. He taught his followers that it was their duty to maintain the topsoil, to study gardening and all the laws of nature and to collaborate with its forces to improve the whole vegetable kingdom and extend it over the surface of the whole earth. He urged his followers to take an active part in developing every aspect of terrestrial nature, plants, trees and all their products.

To encourage this he directed all fathers to plant a fruit tree on every birthday of each of his sons, and on the twenty-first birthday to give the youth the twenty-one fruit trees together with the land on which they grew. This was to be the son's heritage and the father was also commanded to teach the boy all the laws of practical gardening and collaboration with nature so that he could provide for all his own future needs.

The ideal existence for man, Zoroaster taught, is that of the gardener whose work with the soil, air, sunshine and rain keeps him constantly contacting the forces of nature and studying their laws. Study of this greatest book, the book of nature, Zoroaster considered the first step in creating peace and harmony in the kingdom of the Earthly Mother.

The teaching of this same great unity between man and nature appeared in India immediately after the Zend Avesta, in the Vedic philosophy of Brahmanism, in the Upanishads, and later in the teaching of Buddha. The Brahmanic Law of the One, "Thou Art That," (Tat Tvam Asi) expressed the unity of everything, the universe, man, nature. The sages of India were men of the forest, living in complete harmony with all creation.

Berosus, the Chaldean priest, pictured this natural forest way of living.

But the unity between man and nature has been given its most complete and poetic expression in the second chapter of the Essene Gospel of John in which Jesus borrowed his whole terminology from nature to show that man is an integral part of it. Jesus gave a last warning regarding this unity and the necessity of returning to it.

Antediluvian man, the Zoroastrian, the Brahman, the Buddhist, the Essene, all consider the forest and nature to be man's friend and protector, the mother providing all his earthly needs. They never looked upon her as an alien force which had to be fought and conquered as does modern man. The two symbols, the forest and the stone wall, epitomize the vast difference between ancient and modern concepts of nature, between harmonious peacefulness and cooperation and the stone walls of cities, the destruction of plant life, soil, and climate.

Man needs today to learn harmony and peace with nature more than in any other age in history. There are enormous regions over the earth where he is letting the topsoil deteriorate and disappear. Never before has there been such wholesale destruction of forests, not only in one or two countries but all over the five continents. As a consequence of this lack of cooperation with nature the desert areas of the world are increasing, drought is more and more frequent, floods periodically inundate the land. There is an unmistakable deterioration of climate; excessive cold, excessive heat and increasing hordes of insect pests damage crops throughout the world. Instead of following the noble tradition of the Essenes contemporary man fails to recognize the great law of unity and cooperation with nature, and seems bent on deteriorating his heritage, refusing to read the great open book of nature which reveals all the laws of life and shows the way to ever increasing happiness for man.

The Essene teaching shows the only way of organizing man's life on this planet, the only foundation for a healthy humanity, peace with the kingdom of the Earthly Mother.

VII — Peace With the Kingdom of the Heavenly Father

This, the seventh peace, includes all other aspects of peace. The kingdom of the Heavenly Father is the universe, the entire cosmos. It is ruled by the One Law, the totality of all laws. The Heavenly Father is the Law.

Law is everywhere present. It is behind all that is manifest and all that is unmanifest. A stone falls, a mountain forms, seas flow according to law. In accord with law solar systems arise, evolve and disappear. Ideas, sensations, intuitions come and go in man's consciousness according to law. All that is, concrete or abstract, material or immaterial, visible or invisible, is ruled by law, the One Law.

The Law is formless as a mathematical equation is formless. Yet it contains all knowledge, all love, all power. It eternally manifests all truth and all reality. It is man's teacher and friend, showing him all he must do, and know, and be to evolve to the being which he will someday become. The Law guides man in every problem, through every obstacle, telling him always the perfect solution.

Peace with the Law means peace and harmony with the cosmic ocean of all the cosmic forces in the universe. Through this peace, man makes contact with all the superior currents and radiations from all the planets in cosmic space. Through it he is able to attain realization of his unity with all the forces in the universe, those of earth and those from all other planets in the solar system and all galactic systems.

Through this peace he can become united with all the highest values in the universe. Through this peace is awakened the inner intuition which was followed by the mystics and prophets of all ages. Through this peace man contacts his Creator.

This peace completes man's evolution. It brings him total happiness. It is his final goal.

Man is a part of the totality of the universe. He forms an undivided unity with the whole. He thinks himself apart from it because he has become aware of himself as an individual. He has become self-conscious and self-centered beyond the point where self-centeredness is necessary to preserve his life.

This feeling of separation gives rise to his consciousness of lack, of limitation. In thought he has separated himself from the abundance of the universe, shut himself away from the Source of all supply. Supply is material and immaterial, the tangible visible needs for daily life and universal supply of energy, vitality and power, the greatest of which is love.

The Essene considered that man lives in the midst of a field of forces, both terrestrial and planetary, and that his individual evolution progresses to the degree in which he cooperates with these forces. But there are other forces of a superior order with which it is even more important that he is in harmony. These are the spiritual currents in the cosmic ocean of cosmic consciousness. These higher currents do not mingle with the terrestrial and planetary currents. Man by his own efforts, his own will, has to ascend to this cosmic ocean of universal life. Then and then only can he realize his oneness with the Law.

To understand this clearly it is necessary to look at the universe as a whole and to comprehend that it is a totality which includes all its parts, all love, all life, all knowledge, all power, all substance. It is the sum of all substances for out of it all things are formed. It is the sum of all love which is everywhere present, for love is the supreme source and the cohesive force which binds the universe together, in all its parts. Man can no more be apart from this totality than a cell in his body can be apart from his body.

The Essenes spoke of the three parts of man: the material body, the feeling body and the thinking body. But they were always aware that these three parts were not a division in reality for they are all parts of the one higher body, the spiritual body. And this spiritual body is one with and part of all else in the universe.

Man's failure to understand this causes an infinite complexity of false limitations. He not only limits himself in regard to the supply of his material needs, but in regard to his capacities, his abilities, and powers of thinking, feeling and acting. He lives a life of mediocrity because of these false ideas of limitations which he fastens upon himself. Modern science concurs in this, reporting that man has capacities he seldom or never uses. The Essene teaching shows that this condition is caused by his sense of separateness, his self-imposed limitations in which he has become enmeshed by his deviations from the law.

Peace with the kingdom of the Heavenly Father is therefore only possible as man eliminates these deviations and learns to cooperate with the Law, establishing peace and harmony with each of the aspects of the Sevenfold Peace, the acting, thinking and feeling bodies, the family, humanity, culture and nature. Only then can he know the seventh peace, total peace.

The Essenes taught this peace to humanity so that they could overcome all limitations and contact their universal Source, the same Source with which the great masters throughout the ages have united their consciousness when they gave forth their intuitive teachings showing man how to become conscious of the law, understand it, work with it, and manifest it in action.

All history is a record of the self-imposed limitations of man and his efforts to overcome them. These efforts have been made individually, by groups or nations, and in a planetary sense. But they have almost always been made negatively, inharmoniously, through struggle and further deviations from the law. Thus they have bound man in further limitations, further inharmony and further separation in thought from his Source.

The kingdom of the Heavenly Father is always open to him. His return to the universal consciousness, universal supply, is always possible. Once he makes the decision to return and puts forth the persistent effort, he can always go back to the Source, his Heavenly Father, from whom he came and from whom he has never in reality been away.

The great peace of the Essenes teaches man how to go back, how to take the final step that unites him with the cosmic ocean of superior radiations of the whole universe and reach complete union with the Heavenly Father, the totality of all law, the One Law.

This was the ultimate aim of all Essenes and governed their every thought, feeling and action. It is the final aim which all mankind will one day achieve.

THE SEVENFOLD VOW

The vow which the neophyte was required to take before being given the words of the Communions was divided into seven parts in keeping with the Essenes' use of the number seven. The vow was as follows:

1. I want to and will do my best to live like the Tree of Life, planted by the Great Masters of our Brotherhood, with my Heavenly Father who planted the Eternal Garden of the Universe and gave me my spirit; with my Earthly Mother who planted the Great Garden of the Earth and gave me my body; with my brothers who are working in the Garden of our Brotherhood.

2. I want to and will do my best to hold every morning my Communions with the angels of the Earthly Mother, and every evening with the angels of the Heavenly Father, as established by the Great Masters of our Brotherhood.

3. I want to and will do my best to follow the path of the Sevenfold Peace.

4. I want to and will do my best to perfect my Acting Body, my Feeling Body and my Thinking Body, according to the teachings of the Great Masters of our Brotherhood.

5. I will always and everywhere obey with reverence my Master, who gives me the Light of the Great Masters of all times.

6. I will submit to my Master and accept his decision on whatever differences or complaints I may have against any of my brothers working in the Garden of our Brotherhood; and I shall never take any complaint against a brother to the outside world.

7. I will always and everywhere keep secret all the traditions of our Brotherhood which my Master will tell me; and I will never reveal to anyone these secrets without the permission of my Master. I will never claim as my own the knowledge received from my Master and I will always give credit to him for all this knowledge. I will never use the knowledge and power I have gained through initiation from my Master for material or selfish purposes.

"With the coming of day
I embrace my Mother,
with the coming of night
I join my Father,
and with the outgoing of evening and morning
I will breathe Their Law,
and I will not interrupt these Communions
until the end of time."

From "The Manual of Discipline"
of the Dead Sea Scrolls

Chapter 7

Essene Psychology

The Essenes expressed an exceptional knowledge of psychology in their practice of the Communions with the natural and cosmic forces. They knew that man has both a conscious and subconscious mind and were well aware of the powers of each.

In making one group of their Communions the first activity of the morning, they consciously set in motion forces that became the keynote of their whole day. They knew that a thought held strongly enough in the consciousness at the beginning of the day influences the individual throughout his waking hours. The morning Communions consequently opened the mind to harmonious currents which enabled them to absorb specific forms of energy into the physical body.

The evening Communions, performed as the last act in the evening before sleep, applied the same principle. The Essenes knew that these last thoughts influenced the subconscious mind throughout the night, and that the evening Communions therefore put the subconscious into contact with the storehouse of superior cosmic forces. They knew that sleep can thus become a source of deepest knowledge.

The average man experiences this at times, finding a problem solved during sleep and quite often in a way apart from his ordinary trend of thinking. Many scientists, writers and other creative workers have also found that their inventions and ideas have come to them during the night or in the early morning hours.

The knowledge received during sleep is a working of natural law. Although for the majority sleep is little more than a period of detoxication, a means of physiological reparation, for the small minority it represents the psychological perfecting of the individual. The Essenes knew that the higher forces set into action before going to sleep, when the earthly forces of the myriad activities of the day are stilled, would result in the progressive attainment of the lofty objectives of their evening Communions.

They also knew that any negative or inharmonious thought held in their consciousness when they retired would lower their resistance to the negative forces in the outside world.

They had a profound knowledge of the body as well as of the mind. They knew the two could not be separated as they form a dynamic organic unit, and what affects one affects the other. The Essenes antidated psychosomatic medicine by several thousand years.

They knew bodily health had a great deal to do with the receiving of the higher forces, and that a detoxicated organism is more capable of establishing contact with them than is one in which the forces are partially paralyzed by the burden of eliminating bodily poisons during the hours of sleep. The superior revelations which have been brought down to us from antiquity by the great thinkers and teachers were given by those who invariably led very simple and harmonious lives. Their bodies consequently were extremely healthy. It was not merely chance that great revelations of truth were received by the great Masters; their organisms had developed capacities lacked by individuals whose lives have been devoted to more worldly pursuits. The Essene teachings and way of life brought about the development of these capacities.

They paid great attention to the food they ate, that it might harmonize with natural law, but they were equally careful of their diet in thought and emotions. They were fully cognizant that man's subconscious mind is like a sensitized plate registering everything the individual sees or hears, and that it is therefore necessary to prevent all inferior thoughts, such as fear, anxiety, insecurity, hatred, ignorance, egotism and intolerance from entering the gate of the subconscious mind.

The natural law that two things cannot occupy the same space at the same time was clear to them and they knew a person cannot think of two things simultaneously. Therefore if the mind is filled with positive, harmonious thoughts those that are negative and inharmonious cannot lodge in it. Positive, harmonious thoughts must be introduced into the subconscious to replace all inferior ones, just as the cells of the body must constantly be replaced by food, air and water as the old cells are broken down. This was a part of the task accomplished by the Essene Communions, introducing morning, noon and night superior currents of thought and feeling into the thinking and feeling bodies.

The subconscious can be regenerated by a diet of good and harmonious thoughts and feelings administered all during the day, but especially at those moments of borderland consciousness when its receptivity is at its best. When it is thus regenerated it will become a source of energy and harmony to mind and body. It will be a friend sending constructive harmonious messages to every part of the body, causing them to function efficiently.

Certain facts known to the Essenes about introducing a thought or thoughts into the subconscious have been rediscovered by modern psychologists. It is known that when a person is fully conscious, his subconscious mind does not easily accept a purposeful suggestion. And when he is in a subconscious state he cannot of course influence his subconscious consciously. But there are moments when the consciousness is only half submerged in the subconscious, moments such as occur just before going to sleep, just after awaking from sleep, and sometimes when in a state of reverie such as is occasioned by beautiful music or poetry. At such moments the subconscious mind is most receptive to what is given to it.

Many teachings of great religions and practices of ancient and modern philosophical systems, both those of the East and of the West, as well as those of the Essenes, utilize this all-important psychological fact.

The subconscious is dynamic, ever changing, even as are the cells of the body, and it is constantly being fed by the experiences and impressions it receives from the conscious mind. These experiences include all the thoughts and feelings held forcefully enough to create an impression upon it. The traumatic experiences of childhood are those which have been felt with great intensity and fed into the subconscious mind, but never replaced by new and more constructive impressions and experiences.

The subconscious has been defined as the totality of an individual's experiences from birth to the current moment. Every dynamic new experience changes it; and it can be consciously changed according to the degree of the intensity of the impression put into it. The more intense the impression, the more lasting will it be in the subconscious.

Certain other factors were known by the Essenes to govern the acceptance by the subconscious mind of a thought or a feeling. One was that if the conscious mind does not accept the thought as a reality and a possibility, the subconscious will also reject it.

Another was the necessity of projecting the thought to the subconscious without effort, spontaneously. If an effort is made, the fully conscious state is evoked and the subconscious cannot be reached. To act spontaneously and without effort requires complete relaxation of mind and body. This was part of Essene practice.

They accomplished the first step in relaxation by releasing the tensions or contractions of one group of muscles after another over various parts of the body. The second step was shallow breathing. This lessens the oxygen transport in the lungs and thus decreases the activities of the nerves and other parts of the organism since activity and relaxation cannot occur at the same time. The third step was to avoid thought. For man today this is generally not easy. One way of accomplishing it is by imagining, in total darkness and silence, the darkness of black velvet, and thinking of nothing else. Through these three steps the Essenes brought a kind of semiconsciousness into which a new thought or feeling could be readily introduced into the subconscious.

The thought introduced in this way should be rhythmic enough to maintain the state of relaxation and semi-consciousness. And it should have sufficient power to penetrate into the subconscious and be completely accepted as reality. These preconditions of consciously placing thoughts and feelings in the subconscious mind were perfectly met in the practice of the Essene Communions.

It was shown to be entirely up to each individual what is added to the content of his subconscious mind, what kind of new cells he will build into it. He can deviate from the law and be a slave to his subconscious, or he can take an active part in its regeneration.

The Essene's knowledge of the conscious mind was as profound as their understanding of the subconscious. Their concept of psychology was so all-sided they knew the objectives of their Communions could not be attained through intellectual processes alone, but that the force of feelings is also necessary. Knowledge must arouse an emotion before action is produced.

Feeling is not merely an involuntary process, as many people believe. It is a part of the activity of will. The Essenes considered will contains, or is the mechanism of, three factors: thought, feeling and action. This concept can be illustrated in modern terms by comparison to the parts of an automobile. Thought is the steering wheel; feeling is the motor or force; action corresponds to the wheels. To arrive at a particular destination determined upon by will, all three parts must work in collaboration. An objective is thought of, a desire or feeling is aroused, action takes place.

Will can be used to arouse feeling; it frequently must be used if a desired feeling is to be aroused. It can be developed to do this by training. A technique known to the Essenes enabled an individual to use the will in whatever way he might choose.

Few know this; few know their feelings can be mastered. This is because they do not know how to connect their thoughts and their feelings so the desired action results. They may have right knowledge but act in ways contrary to the knowledge; they may have right knowledge of health, for instance, but continue to eat foods that are harmful. But an emotion, such as the fear of pain or death, will cause them to act rightly.

Of the three forces, thought, feeling and action, thought is the youngest, and consequently the weakest influence in man's consciousness. But man is evolving;

his power of thought is increasing steadily. Thought is man's title to nobility. It is a faculty under his individual control; he can think about any subject he wishes. He can control his feelings by thought.

Feelings have a history of hundreds of thousands of years and consequently have built up a much stronger momentum than thought. Consequently they, not thought, govern most of man's actions. Instincts control animals. But man, if he wishes to cease representing the forces of retrogression, must learn to control both instinct and feeling. This he can do through will.

The Essenes believed man should analyze his thoughts and feelings and determine which give him power to carry out a desired action and which paralyze it.

If he does a good deed and analyzes it he can find out what thoughts and feelings prompted his action. He will then understand what kind of thoughts and feelings he should foster.

He will find the deed was not prompted by an abstract thought or a cold intellectual concept. Deeds are prompted by thoughts that have vitality and color, that evoke feeling. Only then do they have enough force to result in action.

Color and vitality are given to thought by creative imagination. Thoughts must create images that are alive. Eastern people have long practiced the art of making thoughts living, full of imagery and pictures. But it is an art that has been much neglected and well nigh forgotten in the West.

Scattered, incoherent thoughts drifting from one thing to another, are only pale wraiths, without life. They are sterile, arousing no feeling, no action. They are valueless.

There is always a feeling behind every action. A right feeling is necessary to produce a right action. Right feelings are sources of energy, harmony and happiness. If they are not sources of these qualities, they are not only valueless; they are dangerous.

Feelings can be placed into one of two categories: those that create energy and those that exhaust it. Through this analysis man can begin to develop will.

By strengthening all the feelings that create energy

and avoiding all those that lead to its exhaustion, the Essenes found that will is acquired. The exercise of will means persevering and patient effort. Through it an individual's superior feelings will gradually create a vast storehouse of energy and harmony; and the inferior feelings, leading to weakness and lack of balance, will eventually be eliminated.

The feeling that creates the greatest energy is love, in all its manifestations, for love is the primordial source of all existence, of all sources of energy, harmony and knowledge. Manifested in terrestrial nature it gives all that is necessary for health. Manifested in the human organism it gives dynamic harmony to all the cells, organs and senses of the organism. Manifested in the consciousness it makes it possible for man to understand cosmic and natural law, including social and cultural laws, and to employ them as sources of harmony and knowledge. Will is the key to the manifestation of this greatest source of energy.

The three enemies of will are dispersion of energy, laziness and sensuality. These three can lead to another formidable enemy of will: disease. Good health is the will's great friend. A dynamic healthy individual commands, and the will obeys; whereas muscular pain or nervous weakness paralyzes the will. This was one of the reasons the Essenes laid such stress on good health and the way of living and thinking that produces health.

The practice of the Communions required continual exercise and use of will. They considered every great value in human culture owes its creation to the exercise of the will, and that true values were only produced by those who use the will. They thoroughly realized the necessity of educating it and considered the key to its education is the direction of the feelings by a powerful creative imagination.

Through their profound understanding of psychological forces the Essene Communions taught man the way to freedom, the way of liberation from blind acceptance of negative conditions either in the physical body or the mind. They showed the way of optimal evolution of both mind and body.

"He assigned to man two spirits with which he
        should walk.
They are the spirits of truth and of falsehood,
truth born out of the spring of Light,
falsehood from the well of darkness.
The dominion of all the children of truth
is in the hands of the Angels of Light
so that they walk in the ways of Light.
The spirits of truth and falsehood struggle within
        the heart of man,
behaving with wisdom and folly.
And according as a man inherits truth
so will he avoid darkness.

"Blessings on all that have cast their lot with the Law,
that walk truthfully in all their ways.
May the Law bless them with all good
and keep them from all evil
and illumine their hearts with insight into the things
        of life
and grace them with knowledge of things eternal."

From "The Manual of Discipline"
of the Dead Sea Scrolls

Chapter 8

Individual Inventory

Thousands of years ago the Essenes practiced a system of psychoanalysis which was much more all-sided than psychoanalysis as practiced today. It is remote from us in time but has a universal quality that modern psychotherapy lacks.

It represents a personal inventory of the Essene ideals of conduct and individual evolution, and can be of the greatest value to contemporary man as a balance sheet of his degree of harmony with the Law.

The Essenes, considering as they did that man lives in the midst of a field of forces, knew that the natural and cosmic forces which surround him and flow through him are superior, positive forces. But they also knew that man by his deviations from the law in thinking, feeling and acting, constantly creates negative, inferior forces in the midst of which he also lives. He is connected with all of these forces and cannot be separated from them; moreover he is always cooperating, consciously or unconsciously with the superior forces or with the inferior ones. He cannot be neutral.

Under this Essene system, which was first practiced at the time of Zoroaster, the individual made a weekly self analysis of his thoughts, words and deeds. This balancing showed the extent to which he was cooperating with or deviating from the superior forces, and gave a cross-section of his character, abilities and physical condition, thus indicating the degree of his evolution in life.

The analysis enabled him to recognize his strong and weak points. By sincerely and vigorously striving to make his thinking, feeling and actions ever better and better, he progressed with the life-time job of self improvement.

There may be some who feel that with all the modern sciences it is unnecessary to go back 8000 years to an ancient teaching. But it is a question how much the developments of science have accomplished in increasing human happiness and well being. The general insecurity and neurosis of the present day and the widespread economic and social unrest give a definitely negative answer. Man has gained an enormous amount of theoretical knowledge in the framework of his scientific culture but this has not increased his happiness or individual evolution. It has not served to connect him with the universe, the cosmic system, or to show him his place and role in it.

Without such knowledge man cannot follow the path of optimal evolution for himself or for the planet.

The present day neurosis is caused by man's current deviations from the law of harmony with natural and cosmic forces. If a man tries his best to live in harmony with them he will never develop neurosis.

Psychology today tends to emphasize only one or two of these natural forces. Freud, for instance, considered deviations from the law of the natural force of sex caused man's inharmony; others have concentrated on other forms of deviation. But the system practiced in Zoroaster's time considered harmony with all the natural and cosmic forces to be necessary for all-around health and psychological balance. Its superiority over other systems rests in its all-sidedness and universality.

The job of self-improvement, it shows, has to be carried on day by day, by the individual himself. Psychoanalysis, on the other hand, depends largely on the analyst, for the person being analyzed assumes a somewhat passive role. In the Zoroastrian method the individual's achievement of harmony is the life-time task of the individual, not some one else's job to be completed in a couple of years or less.

The sixteen elements used in the system embrace every aspect of human life. They correspond, in a degree, to the fourteen forces symbolized by the Essene Tree of Life. It was not the purpose of the Essenes, either in the time of Zoroaster or later, to divide the natural and cosmic forces into any rigid or artificial pattern, but simply to consider them in such ways as would express most clearly their value and utilization in man's life.

Perfection was not demanded in the analysis, but the individual was urged to strive continually to improve his relationship to each of the sixteen forces and to achieve ever greater harmony and utilization of their powers and energies. The individual who does this will enjoy an actively creative life bringing him the highest measure of happiness and service to others. The one who continues to deviate will find life becoming less and less interesting and rewarding while misery and frustration will become increasingly great.

The teachings of the Essenes gave man a clear knowledge of his place and role in the universe and their method of weekly self-analysis enabled them to know how clearly they understood the teaching and how thoroughly they were practicing it and following the path of their individual evolution.

Of the sixteen forces that were utilized in making the analysis, eight belonged to the earthly forces and eight to the cosmic ones. The earthly forces were the sun, water, air, food, man, earth, health and joy. The cosmic powers were power, love, wisdom, the preserver, the Creator, eternal life, work and peace.

The analysis considered each of the forces from three different aspects:

1. Is the power or force understood

2. Does the individual feel the significance of the force deeply and sincerely

3. Is the power used continually and in the best possible way

THE EARTHLY FORCES

The following are the meanings and uses of the earthly forces.

1. **The sun** is a very important source of energy and its solar power is to be contacted and utilized to the utmost every day in the form that is best for the health and well being of the individual.

2. **Water** is an essential element of life. It is to be used in the proper way in diet and a bath in water is to be taken every morning throughout the year.

3. **Air** has a tremendous role in the health of the body and as much time as possible is to be spent outdoors breathing pure fresh air and utilizing the energies of the atmosphere for health.

4. **Food** is to be of the right kind and taken in the right amount to supply another vital force to the organism.

5. **Man** was considered to be a force representing each one's right and responsibility toward his own evolution. Each individual is to use every moment to further his progress in life and it is a job which no one can do for him. He is to know, and understand, his own potentialities and find the most practical way of developing and utilizing them in the service of mankind.

6. **Earth** represents the two aspects of the generative force which creates more abundant life on the planet. The one creates life from the soil, producing the trees and all vegetation. The other manifests in the sexual energies in man. The individual is to understand and utilize the most optimal ways of growing plants and food, and of a harmonious sexual life.

7. **Health** is dependent upon man's harmonious relationship with all the forces of earth, with the sun, water, air, food, man, earth and joy. The individual is to realize the importance of good health for his own sake and for the sake of others; and he is to practice all ways of improving his health, in thinking, feeling and acting.

8. **Joy** is man's essential right and he is to perform all his daily activities with a deep feeling of joy surging

within him and radiating around him, understanding its great importance for himself and others.

These are the forces of nature which man is to learn to understand and utilize. The following eight powers of the cosmos are even more important in man's life, for he cannot live in complete harmony with the earthly forces unless he is also in harmony with the heavenly powers.

THE COSMIC FORCES

1. **Power** is manifested continually through man's actions and deeds, both of which are the result of his cooperation or lack of cooperation with all other powers and forces, in accord with the iron law of cause and effect. The individual is to understand the importance of good deeds; and he is to realize that his personality, position and environment in life are the result of his past deeds, even as his future will be exactly what his present deeds make it. He is therefore to strive at all times to perform good deeds that express harmony with the laws of both nature and the cosmos.

2. **Love** is expressed in the form of gentle and kind words to others, which affect the individual's own health and happiness as well as that of others. Sincere love toward all beings is to be manifested by harmonious feelings and words.

3. **Wisdom** is manifested in the form of good thoughts and it is man's privilege and right to increase his knowledge and understanding in every way possible so that he may think only good thoughts. He is to seek to grow in wisdom so as to understand more and more the cosmic order and his own role in it. Only by attaining a degree of wisdom can an individual learn to hold only good thoughts in his consciousness and to refuse to entertain negative, destructive thoughts about any person, place, condition or thing.

4. **Preservation** of values concerns the power to preserve all that is useful and of true value, whether a tree, plant, house, relationship between people or harmony in any form. When anyone destroys, or lets any good thing go to waste, deteriorate or be damaged, whether material or

immaterial, he is cooperating with the negative destructive forces of the world. Every opportunity is to be used to prevent damage to whatever has value.

5. **Creation** signifies the necessity for man to use his creative powers, since his role on the planet is to continue the work of the Creator. He is therefore to try to do something original and creative, something new and different, as often as he can, whether it is an invention of some kind, a work of art, or anything which will benefit others.

6. **Eternal Life** concerns man's sincerity with himself and others in all he does and with all those whom he meets. He is to be deeply sincere in analyzing his relationship, his understanding and utilization of all the forces of nature and the cosmos; and he is to make every effort to evaluate himself honestly as he actually is without rationalizing or justifying the things he does or says or thinks.

7. **Work** is the precondition of many other values. It means the performance of one's daily tasks with care and efficiency. It is an individual's contribution to society and a precondition of happiness for all concerned, for when one person does not perform his work properly, others have to do it. Man is to learn to have a deep feeling of satisfaction in his work so that he may return to society all he receives from it.

8. **Peace** is to be created and maintained by every individual within and around himself that he may be an instrument in helping to prevent inharmony, enmity and wars, since the condition of the whole of humanity depends upon the condition of its atoms, the individuals who compose it. The individual is to feel deeply the need for this inner peace and to do all he can to establish and maintain it wherever he is.

The person who evaluates himself according to these sixteen elements of life will know clearly wherein his personal development may be improved, and in what ways he can help more fully in the evolution of humanity.

By so doing he will move further toward his final goal, the goal toward which all mankind is moving, union with the Heavenly Father.

"I have reached the inner vision
and through Thy spirit in me
I have heard Thy wondrous secret.
Through Thy mystic insight
Thou hast caused a spring of knowledge
to well up within me,
a fountain of power,
pouring forth living waters,
a flood of love
and of all-embracing wisdom
like the splendor of eternal Light."

From "The Book of Hymns"
of the Dead Sea Scrolls

93

THE ESSENE WAY: *AN INVITATION*

If you found this book meaningful, you may be interested to learn more about THE ESSENE WAY, a renaissance of the ageless values of the first century Essenes, translated into creative and constructive 20th century life styles.

Over the years, thousands upon thousands of truth-seekers from all over the world have written to us, asking for the opportunity to study and put into practice the Essene teachings in a harmonious framework, in the company of those motivated by similar ideas and ideals. In response to this need, *The Essene Way,* in cooperation with Academy Books, Publishers, now conducts an annual Essene Seminar and Workshop, attended every summer by students from all over the United States and abroad.

If you would like to know more about next summer's Essene Seminar and Workshop, or if you are interested in a comprehensive home study program, please write to *The Essene Way,* care of Academy Books, Publishers, 3085 Reynard Way, San Diego, California 92103, for our usual *spring* announcement.

The Essene Seminar also provides training for future teachers and ministers. We cordially invite those who are seriously interested to write to *The Essene Way.*

Peace be with you!

SELECTED BOOKS BY EDMOND BORDEAUX SZEKELY
ON THE ESSENE WAY OF BIOGENIC LIVING

GUIDE TO THE ESSENE WAY OF BIOGENIC LIVING. All-sided practical techniques of adaptation of the ancient Essene teachings to our 20th century daily life. *Biogenic Living in World Perspectives, Biogenic Nutrition, Biogenic Living, Biogenic Dwelling, Biogenic Meditation, Biogenic Sexual Fulfillment, Biogenic Psychology and Self-Analysis, Biogenic Education, the Essene-Biogenic World Movement, the International Biogenic Society.* The "ten-books-in-one" Biogenic Encyclopedia. Richly illustrated throughout. $ 8.80

THE DISCOVERY OF THE ESSENE GOSPEL OF PEACE: The Essenes & the Vatican	4.80
SEARCH FOR THE AGELESS, I: My Unusual Adventures on the Five Continents in Search for the Ageless	7.80
SEARCH FOR THE AGELESS, II: The Great Experiment	8.80
SEARCH FOR THE AGELESS, III: The Chemistry of Youth	7.50
THE TENDER TOUCH: BIOGENIC FULFILLMENT	5.50
THE BIOGENIC REVOLUTION: The 1977 International Essene Seminar	9.50
BIOGENIC REDUCING: THE WONDER WEEK	3.80
THE ESSENE BOOK OF CREATION	4.50
THE ESSENE JESUS	4.50
THE ESSENE BOOK OF ASHA: JOURNEY TO THE COSMIC OCEAN	7.50
THE ZEND AVESTA OF ZARATHUSTRA	4.80
ARCHEOSOPHY, A NEW SCIENCE	3.80
THE ESSENE ORIGINS OF CHRISTIANITY	7.50
THE ESSENES, BY JOSEPHUS AND HIS CONTEMPORARIES	1.80
THE ESSENE TEACHINGS OF ZARATHUSTRA	1.80
THE ESSENE SCIENCE OF LIFE	2.80
THE ESSENE CODE OF LIFE	2.80
THE ESSENE SCIENCE OF FASTING AND THE ART OF SOBRIETY	2.80
THE COSMOTHERAPY OF THE ESSENES	2.80
THE LIVING BUDDHA: A Comparative Study of Buddha and Yoga	4.50
TOWARD THE CONQUEST OF THE INNER COSMOS	5.80
JOURNEY THROUGH A THOUSAND MEDITATIONS	9.50
FATHER, GIVE US ANOTHER CHANCE: Survival Through Creative Simplicity	5.80
THE ECOLOGICAL HEALTH GARDEN AND THE BOOK OF SURVIVAL	3.95
MAN IN THE COSMIC OCEAN	2.80
THE DIALECTICAL METHOD OF THINKING	1.95
THE EVOLUTION OF HUMAN THOUGHT	1.95
THE SOUL OF ANCIENT MEXICO	7.50
THE NEW FIRE: THE RENEWAL OF LIFE	4.80
DEATH OF THE NEW WORLD	4.80
ANCIENT AMERICA: PARADISE LOST	4.80
PILGRIM OF THE HIMALAYAS: The Discovery of Tibetan Buddhism	1.95
MESSENGERS FROM ANCIENT CIVILIZATIONS: Ancient Migrations	2.50
SEXUAL HARMONY	3.50
LUDWIG VAN BEETHOVEN, PROMETHEUS OF THE MODERN WORLD	1.75
BOOKS, OUR ETERNAL COMPANIONS	2.50
THE FIERY CHARIOTS: The Mysterious Brotherhood of the Dead Sea	4.80
CREATIVE WORK: KARMA YOGA	1.95
THE ART OF STUDY: THE SORBONNE METHOD	2.50
COSMOS, MAN AND SOCIETY	5.80
I CAME BACK TOMORROW: The 20th Century Nightmare and the Essene Dream	2.80
BROTHER TREE: A Charming Ecological Parable for Children of All Ages	2.80
CREATIVE EXERCISES FOR HEALTH AND BEAUTY	2.95
THE BOOK OF LIVING FOODS	2.95
SCIENTIFIC VEGETARIANISM	2.50
THE CONQUEST OF DEATH	1.95
HEALING WATERS: Fifty European Spa Treatments at Home	3.50
THE PREVENTIVE DIET FOR HEART AND OVERWEIGHT	2.50

Please write for complete descriptive catalogue to
INTERNATIONAL BIOGENIC SOCIETY
Apartado 372, Cartago, Costa Rica, Central America